M000203056

HE CALLS ME
Bethany

BARBARA HOLMES

Trilogy Christian Publishers
A Wholly Owned Subsidary of Trinity Broadcasting Network
2442 Michelle Drive
Tustin, CA 92780

Copyright © 2020 by Barbara Holmes

All rights reserved, including the right to reproduce this book or portions thereof in any form whatsoever.

For information, address Trilogy Christian Publishing
Rights Department, 2442 Michelle Drive, Tustin, Ca 92780.
Trilogy Christian Publishing/ TBN and colophon are trademarks of Trinity Broadcasting Network.

For information about special discounts for bulk purchases, please contact Trilogy Christian Publishing.

Manufactured in the United States of America

Trilogy Disclaimer: The views and content expressed in this book are those of the author and may not necessarily reflect the views and doctrine of Trilogy Christian Publishing or the Trinity Broadcasting Network.

10 9 8 7 6 5 4 3 2 1

Library of Congress Cataloging-in-Publication Data is available.

ISBN 978-1-64773-328-5 (Print Book)
ISBN 978-1-64773-329-2 (ebook)

Scripture quotations marked KJV are taken from the King James Version of the Bible. Public domain.

Scripture quotations marked (CEV) are from the Contemporary English Version: Contemporary English Version, Second Edition (CEV®) © 2006 American Bible Society. All rights reserved.

Scripture quotations marked CJB are taken from the Complete Jewish Bible. Public domain.

Scripture quotations marked (ERV) are taken from the HOLY BIBLE: EASY-TO-READ VERSION © 2001 by World Bible Translation Center, Inc. and used by permission.

Scriptures marked as "(GNT)" are taken from the **Good News Translation—Second Edition** © 1992 by American Bible Society. Used by permission.

Scripture quotations marked HCSB are been taken from the Holman Christian Standard Bible®, Copyright © 1999, 2000, 2002, 2003 by Holman Bible Publishers. Used by permission. Holman Christian Standard Bible®, Holman CSB®, and HCSB® are federally registered trademarks of Holman Bible Publishers.

Scripture quotations marked NASB are taken from the New American Standard Bible® (NASB), Copyright © 1960, 1962, 1963, 1968, 1971, 1972, 1973, 1975, 1977, 1995 by The Lockman Foundation. Used by permission. www.Lockman.org.

Scripture quotations marked NIV are taken from the Holy Bible, New International Version®, NIV®. Copyright © 1973, 1978, 1984, 2011 by Biblica, Inc.™ Used by permission of Zondervan. All rights reserved worldwide. www.zondervan.com. The "NIV" and "New International Version" are trademarks registered in the United States Patent and Trademark Office by Biblica, Inc.™

Scripture quotations marked (NKJV) taken from The Holy Bible, New King James Version®. Copyright © 1982 by Thomas Nelson, Inc. All rights reserved.

Scripture quotations marked NLT are taken from the Holy Bible, New Living Translation, copyright © 1996, 2004, 2015 by Tyndale House Foundation. Used by permission of Tyndale House Publishers, Inc., Carol Stream, Illinois 60188. All rights reserved.

Scripture quotations marked (NOG) taken from GOD'S WORD®, © 1995 God's Word to the Nations. Used by permission of Baker Publishing Group.

Scripture quotations marked TPT are from The Passion Translation®. Copyright © 2017, 2018 by Passion & Fire Ministries, Inc. Used by permission. All rights reserved. ThePassionTranslation.com.

I dedicate this book to my two grandmamas. Even in abuse, segregation, and forgetfulness, they trusted in Jesus. I dedicate this to my momma who taught me how to give my faith legs to run ahead of my fears. I also dedicate this to Paul who calls forth my beautiful every day. And to my little lambs; Lynette, Josiah, John and grandchildren. Always remember what God has done; and pass it on.

Deuteronomy 11:13-21

Introduction

Every one of us will have a season in our life when we will go through difficult times. Those times can mess with our minds, our emotions, and affect how we see ourselves and God. It doesn't matter what trauma we are facing; Jesus is calling us out of our pain and into His love. He calls us all by name. Nothing can separate us from the love of Jesus. In our world, many people are hurting, and don't know who they really are. They carry open wounds from their battles that are infected with lies from the enemy of their soul. In addition, many people are unaware of what God's voice sounds like and looks like in their lives. My road towards understanding my identity in God, and learning how to hear His voice in my life, has been full of beautiful moments of pain, growth, and freedom.

Many of my experiences growing up would have destroyed me had it not been for the Word of God. He has shown Himself faithful and has many times supernaturally carried me through brutal seasons of my life. In this book, I share with you thirty-one stories highlighting some of my experiences. I will describe some of the evil I lived through as a little girl, and how I overcame it by the Word of God and the power of His Holy Spirit. I will also tell you some of my journey of learning how to understand God's voice and act in obedience to it. Every story comes from the archives of my life, and each one is true.

Names in the stories were changed to protect my friends and family. I believe that these stories will bolster your faith to saturate yourself with the Word of God. They will give insight on overcoming the enemy's attacks on the garden of your soul and will encourage you to live a deeper Spirit-led life. These stories are very raw and honest. Each story can be read as a stand-alone if you wish. The verses in the stories come from my personal arsenal of battle verses that I use when I wage war against the enemy or need to remind myself of God's heart towards me. I often use the phrase "Holy Spirit" instead of "The Holy Spirit." This is because of the personal way I think of God's spirit. It's more comfortable for me to say it that way, although it may sound a bit weird for some readers at first. In addition, I use both the names "Jesus" and "Yeshua" for Jesus. My ultimate prayer for you in the reading of this book is that these pieces from my experiences with Jesus would:

o   Inspire the discovery and understanding of God's point of view of who you are and what He is calling you to.
o   Encourage faithfulness to God's Word and recognition of the faithfulness of God in your own life.
o   Increase your expectation to hear from the Lord, which requires learning how He speaks to you.
o   Impart courage to allow our Creator to define Himself and what He's capable of, rather than Him being defined by boundaries placed on Him.

Remember, nothing can separate us from His love. Nothing (Romans 8:35-38, NLT).

BEGINNING

Falling in Love

"Whenever I am afraid, I will trust
in You." (Psalm 56:3, NKJV)

It was the first time I realized that He loved me. Not just a causal "you are cute and you make me smile" kind of love, but the "I would die a thousand deaths for you" kind. I was around five, almost six years old lying in my bed. Afraid. Not so much of who, but of what. I really didn't understand who I was to God. I had heard all the right words in church, but my heart had not fully connected to my identity as a beloved and treasured daughter of the creator of all things. Of course, it is hard to have that kind of reality when sin and the effects of it become so normalized in your life. The nights for me as a child were the worst. The nights were a hot time for demons in my room during those days. Yucky things in the long dark nights that came with despair and left me near terrified. I needed to know that I was not alone. That's when He came. I know it sounds cliché to say, but my life has never been the same since. Let me tell you my story of falling in love.

My home life was pretty good from the street view. I was living with my father, mother, and a baby brother. My family lived in Texas, and both my parents had grown up there for most of their years. You may have heard that Texas has a big personality, and we were Texans through and through. We had a home, we had a yard to play in, we even had a few pets. My mom, a teacher, was the light of our home. She carried the heavy burdens of raising us, and she was always doing her best to love past hurts and traumas incurred throughout our years together in our home. Every family has ups and downs. Ours was no different in that sense, but it was the depth of which those downs would go that created so much of our family pain. Family secrets and the fear of admitting the issues that swirled in my home created a false sense of security there. I learned at a very young age that just because someone says they love you doesn't mean it's really love they have. But, in the defense of anyone who loves so brokenly that it is hurting others, you probably haven't learned how to love God's way. In fact, you probably don't even truly believe just how passionate God's love is for you in spite of what you are doing or have done. And you are not alone. As a child, I learned a lot about what love was through my mom, what love wasn't through others, and what lies were from my world.

My parents were leaders in our community. My momma, who was an urban missionary before meeting my dad, had a lot of experience in leadership. My mom was a founding member of a small youth mission group and they served many years seeing many young inner-city children come to Christ and be discipled for the kingdom of God. She also sang soprano in a Christian singing group for a season of her life. She was, and still is, a passionate and active follower of Jesus. My father, a person naturally bent towards leading, found my mother's skills and gifts very helpful towards helping him in his own personal goals. He professed a love for Christ and sought ways to work in Christian ministry throughout his life.

More than sharing the gospel, I believe he just liked power. However, it wasn't always obvious to others. My father, a very social and friendly man, worked as a salesman for his day job. He had a God-given gift for connecting with people. He used his gift to accomplish his goals, sounding honest and trustworthy. He lied often to family and friends, but very few people knew it, because he seemed so honest.

My family was like a house with fake walls. Though my mom was truly kind, honest, and well respected, the lies my father lived in created pressure in our home as leaders to keep the nasty, icky secrets inside and never let them out. My dad knew how to fit in church life, and I genuinely believe he wanted to be a better dad and husband. My heart tells me that he struggled deeply with depression, guilt, and shame. However, his addiction to pornography, and his perverse thought life had become a playground for spiritual foul play long before I was born. Some people assume idolatry has gone away, but many a human has the same old idols, just with new names. My dad was no exception. Though my home was full of the prayers of many, it was also a portal for demonic activity, the likes of which I wonder if should even say.

For me in those days, morning was the best time. We had a pretty busy and routine lifestyle. I went to a Christian school. My mother would drive me every day. My principle Mrs. Hills and her husband Hilton, an ex-athlete, were my favorite teachers there. I trusted them as much as I trusted my mom. My friends at my school were consistent and faithful. My bestie Pam and I knew all the secret spots on the playground and the perfect trees for a girl's club and club meetings. Pam was my safe space at school. She wasn't perfect, but neither was I. We got into trouble sometimes in silly ways. But she was someone who I could trust to be consistent in her affections towards me, and she valued me deeply as a friend. Besides enjoying school, my mom and I would spend a lot of time together after school hanging out. Momma would play dolls with me and she would take me on most of her outings in town. She would regularly take my brothers and me to the library for various events. Sometimes, she would take me out to eat or to a snack shack to get a street taco or something.

My mom worked a lot at church, and much of our free time was spent there. While at church, I spent my time with my favorite cousin Christie Love and my aunties. Everyone was an aunt or uncle at our church. You really didn't have to be blood related to be family. I carry that way of living with me today. I loved my time at church. That's where my greatest community was. My family and friends there were a huge part of my life influences, and I can say that some of my favorite memories were at church. Church for me was a safe place. No demons attacked me there. I was in a house flooded with constant prayer at church. It was such a contrast to the late night hours when those monsters seemed the closest. Therefore, the morning hours in the light of day were my favorite times, though that's not to say that some of those demons didn't lurk their nasty heads out during the day. On occasions they did, but the night was different. At night as I laid down, the demons would literally hover above my bed snarling with their twisted ash-gray faces. They had small horns on their heads and they sometimes drooled through their strange teeth. They looked gaunt, yet you could see every detail of all their muscles.

Oh, how I feared them. They wouldn't touch me, though they seemed to try. I would cry silent tears in terror almost every night as this was happening. I didn't tell my mom what was happening. Honestly, I really didn't think she would believe me. I had tried to tell her about it before, but she told me it was my imagination. I don't blame her. That is what any mom under normal circumstances would assume. I would often sing the third verse to "Away in A Manger" as a prayer over and over while lying in bed;

> "Be near me, Lord Jesus, I ask Thee to stay,
> Close by me forever, and love me, I pray!
> Bless all the dear children in Thy tender care
> And take us to heaven, to Live with Thee there."

I would close my eyes and sing it until the monsters went to the corner of the room. Then I would wrap my blanket tight around my neck and partially over my head and peak out to keep watch until I went to sleep. Some nights, more nights than I'd like to say, my dad would come in my room. Those nights, he was the monster. I felt so confused about my dad. But I knew those demons had something to do with him. Sometimes I saw some them with him in the daytime. I felt so unprotected in the same space as my father. I knew God loved me, at least I thought I knew. I had begun to think that maybe God's love was like my Dad's. I felt so confused and began to pray for something different. A different dad maybe. A different life perhaps. In the daytime I would imagine all kinds of other lives I could have outside of what I had. I wanted God to take me away from all of it.

It was on a night when my dad was not there in my room while I was praying my third verse of "Away in a Manger" watching the demons above me do their normal "I'm gonna get ya" routine, that

Jesus appeared in my room. I had always been told up to that point that He was always with me, but that night I saw Him with my own eyes. It was bright, like a shining white light in my room. I then noticed that I had two very large angels, one on each side of me, each having one of their very big and strong arms wrapped around me. In that moment, I could see clearly why those demons could never touch me. This revelation of the actual presence of Jesus with me pierced my soul. I was floored and overwhelmed by His God-ness. He really was God, and He was with me. As I felt the strength of the angel's arms around me, and as I gazed into the face of Jesus, I forgot to even pay attention to the demons. It was as if they were rendered powerless. I became lost in His love. I knew He had heard my song and my heart burned with a deep fire, a passion to love Him back. I noticed the demons had left my room, but my angels were still there. They stayed at my side. Jesus also stayed. He just stood at my bed. He didn't leave me. He wasn't there to pilfer the innocence of my soul or desecrate my body. He wasn't there to criticize me or tell me how I would become nothing. He wasn't there to beat me. He was simply loving me. A real kind of love from a Father I only then realized I was just beginning to understand. I rolled over and closed my eyes in peace, overcome with how much love I was feeling.

It was very apparent to me as a five-year-old that all I knew about love was wrong. I was elated at the possibilities in my life from having Jesus with me like this. This is my first memory of stepping beyond the Christian doctrine of God's love and falling into the reality of it. For me, it was the beginning of a journey that would take me into deep intimacy with my Savior and to what He calls me. I went to bed thinking to myself, I would die a thousand deaths for you Jesus. You vanquished my enemy. You captured my heart. I am Yours forever. There I was, a powerless little girl who felt like I couldn't talk to anyone about what was going on, and He showed Himself to me. In that moment, I went from feeling like an insignificant human to a princess with my own personal angelic guards. My identity in Jesus was becoming clearer to me. The way His love radiated every space of me that night…it has never left me. It was the first time that I truly realized just how much He loved me. I have been falling in love with Him ever since.

Seeds of Learning

"Let us not become weary in doing good for
at the proper time we will reap a harvest if
we do not give up." (Galatians 6:9, NIV)

After my pre-school years, my mother decided that a Christian school was best for me. My parents then enrolled me in what would be one of the most influential educational seasons of my young life. This was not because of the academics, though the academics were good there. No, it was because of the character building and foundational faith in God that developed in me during my years there. My mom had foresight for my life that was far bigger than mine during those years. And by faith, she set out to work out a financial plan to send me to that Christian school. However, my dad wasn't always on board with having a school expense in the budget. This was especially true during the years when money was tight for my family. It was during one of these seasons when Lady Diane, a single independent woman who was passionate about missions, service, and children, stepped in and helped my mom keep me at my beloved school. God was using that Christian school to help me develop a God-perspective of who I was to Him. Holy Spirit used Lady Diane to help me stay there for the full duration that was appointed for me to be there. Later, I would understand the great sacrifice that Lady Diane made and the seeds of learning that would grow in me for years to come.

Lady Diane was a beautiful lady. She had long dark hair. Some said she was part Native American. She looked it for sure. She had all the beauty of a Native princess. She wasn't very tall. Lady Diane was only a little taller than me even when I was a kid, but her spirit was great and wide. She was one of the strongest women I had ever met. I loved her so. She was my teacher in VBS and sometimes at Sunday school. Lady Diane also taught many other children. Education was very important to her. Not just academics but learning the Word of God. She could always be seen where the kids were. She had a zeal for spreading the love of Yeshua. She worked as a missionary her whole life in neighborhoods that some would have looked over. Lady Diane never overlooked a child. She dropped seeds of learning wherever she went. She was tough, but so kind to others. Lady Diane's tentmaking skill was teaching. I believe she realized how important my Christian school was to me. When my parents told me I would no longer go there, she saw how sad I was. She jumped right in to help my mother financially so I could continue my education there.

I was able to continue at my Christian school all the way through eighth grade. Then, out of nowhere, we moved to Washington state. All those years at my Christian school would not have happened without the love and support of Lady Diane. I needed every one of those years I spent there. Despite the troubles I had at home with my Dad, I had found a very trustworthy man, Mr. Hills, who ministered to my wounds through those years in such a deep way. God was using Mr. Hills and my time there to help me understand His love towards me. In addition, this school had a strong focus on getting the Word of God in your heart, not just in your head. I don't think I fully appreciated the impact Lady Diane's contribution was having on my life while I was going to the Christian school. Although, I began to realize it when I began going to the public high school in Washington. I called upon every Bible verse I had taken to heart during my time in high school. I became genuinely grateful for the time I had to grow and develop at my Christian school, especially the time to develop the relationship I had with God. I doubt I would have been the student I was at that high school had it not been for my Christian school years and the word of God in me.

Lady Diane fought with cancer throughout her life. While she was living, I dreamed that she was on an ice-skating rink and all her family and friends were watching from the stands. An announcer declared that Lady Diane was going to perform her last swan dance.

In the dream, she then begins to skate the most amazing dance I had ever seen. Then, in her last spin, she just disappeared and was gone. Everyone stood and cheered with tears in their eyes. Then the family and friends left the stands and went through a door into a reception hall. I tried to go through the door, but I couldn't for some reason. I could only look in. The year I had that dream was around the time of my family reunion. My mother, my youngest brother, my two sons (one being in the womb), and I flew down south to see family and friends at that year's reunion. It was a lively time. Lady Diane was there of course. She wouldn't have missed it. Everyone danced and celebrated, especially since my Aunt Cookie had just passed. My Aunt Cookie was beloved by so many, including my oldest son. He was quite fond of her. We were all so grateful to be together and to enjoy the company of everyone we loved.

Occasions like reunions always remind us of the importance of each other. I love these events because I get to see people that I don't get to see often, like Christie Love, my bestie. Christie Love and I, along with my youngest brother, oldest son and baby in the womb, spent a day at NASA. We also took a riverboat ride with everyone who came to the reunion. I spent a lot of time with Lady Diane on that trip. I was near six months pregnant at that time and was getting around much slower. Lady Diane was also getting around a bit slower. So, we would take our time getting around as slowly as suited us. I had the dream in my mind as well. I really didn't know what God was showing me, at least I didn't really want to think it was what I felt it was. In addition, Lady Diane said she was doing fine every time I asked her how she was. Therefore, I convinced myself that I really didn't understand what God had shown me.

When the reunion was over, everyone went home. Life got back to normal. It was a short time later that my mom got a phone call that Lady Diane was dying in a hospital, unresponsive. As it turns out, Lady Diane's cancer had returned and had spread throughout her body. Even though she had known it at the reunion, she didn't tell anyone. She died, and although she never had birth children, she left behind a very long line of descendants who would not be the amazing people they are had it not been for the sacrifices she made for them, serving them with her gifts, time, money, and prayers. I wasn't able to go to the funeral. I was too far along in my pregnancy to fly. That's why in the dream I couldn't go through the door where the reception was.

So many children who are now adults are better, healthier, and living a blessed life, in part, because of Lady Diane. Her love well overflowed to so many during her lifetime. And such a beautiful life it was. Her testimony lives on in the children and adults whose lives she touched. Perhaps you have had the opportunity to share your skills, resources, and time with others. You may never know the longevity or impact of what you do in your lifetime. I encourage you not to grow weary in doing good things. God sees and knows how to use every gift you give for bigger outcomes than you could comprehend. Lady Diane was a mother to many, and a servant to all. Lady Diane was a sower of seeds wherever she went. She leaves a legacy that is grand and widespread. I am so grateful for the seeds of learning sown in my life. I wouldn't be who I am otherwise.

Of Spankings and Shopping

"How joyful are those whose lawless
acts are forgiven and whose sins are
covered!" (Romans 4:7, HCSB)

"Look with wonder at the depth of the
Father's marvelous love that he has lavished
on us! He has called us and made us his very
own beloved children. The reason the world
doesn't recognize who we are is that they
didn't recognize him." (1 John 3:1 TPT)

Of all the schools I went to after eighth grade through Highschool, that Christian school in Texas was by far my favorite. The principal at the school was Mrs. Hills. Actually, when I was in kindergarten, she was the vice-principal. She became the principal a year or two later. I was in her wedding before she became Mrs. Hills, and I spent a lot of time with her. When she married Hilton, an athlete, he joined right in on spoiling me. They really did treat me thoughtfully, like loving parents. Being with them at my school was, without a doubt, one of the safer places for me those ten years of my life, and the adventures I had with Mr. and Mrs. Hills I shall never forget.

One of my favorite times at my Christian school was recess. I never knew what was going to happen. Most kids would look forward to the games on the playground. I looked forward to the possibility of going shopping with Mrs. Hills. She would sometimes use that time to pick up things for the school in town or run a few errands. From time to time, she would take me and sometimes a friend as well. It felt like girl's time out together. She'd stop to pick up something to eat and always gave me a special snack. One of my favorite trips was when she took me coat shopping. She was buying a winter coat, and she let me help her pick it out. I loved those outings. I always felt so special, like I was her only one. She was firm, but she was always very sweet to me. It's hard to top a principal like that.

Sometimes I would get in trouble. Not big trouble, but my school had lots of rules to keep some basic order amongst the students. There was the 6-inch rule to ensure that boys and girls maintained proper conduct, the dress code rules to create a sense of unity in modesty in how everyone dressed, the "no looking over your divider" rule so students could focus, and rules associated with scoring your paces so no one would feel tempted to cheat. On occasion, I might break a rule or two without trying to, and, depending on which rules were bent and how many times they were broken, it meant a trip to the office to get popped. That's right. A spanking with a paddle. When I got in trouble, I can honestly say it was mostly on accident. I really worked hard to follow all the school rules. Mr. and Mrs. Hills knew that. Once when I was in elementary, someone said that I cursed. No one cursed around me so, if I had done so, I had no idea it was a curse word. I was promptly taken to the pop room. I was so scared, I thought I was in big trouble. I started to cry really hard and Mr. Hills put his arms around me and said, "Barb, be strong. Be strong!" I guess that's how former football players talk to little girls. He told me not to worry. Then he took the paddle and popped the table. I then realized that he had no intention of paddling me. I was so relieved. He told me to look sad on the way back to class. He gave me some tissue to blow my nose and sent me out. He was a softy. I wonder if he ever spanked anybody.

During another occasion in elementary, I really did get into honest-to-goodness trouble. Pam and I were hanging out in Mrs. Hills office, probably waiting to go out with her or something. Pam was my best friend at school and she and I did everything together, including getting into some creative activity, sometimes referred to as trouble. Mrs. Hills wasn't in there at the time, and we got bored. Mrs. Hills often kept a long incense stick burning in her office on a shelf. She also always had a box of tissue paper on her desk. Next to the desk was a small black waste basket that was filled with used tissue. Pam and I got the great idea to see how well one of those soft tissues would burn. You probably are saying to yourself, "This is not a good idea." And you would be right. However, we were bored kids in the principal's office. It's only natural to come up with crazy, and possibly dangerous, ideas like testing the burn time of a soft facial tissue. The plan was that I would pull a tissue out of the box and use the incense stick to light it up. Pam would stand by and take mental notes on what happened. I grabbed a tissue paper from the box, put it towards the burning incense, and instantly the facial tissue became devoured by flames. Obviously, I dropped it. I didn't want to get burned. The burning tissue fell into the waste bin, which, as you remember, was full of used tissue. Pam and I were frantic! We grabbed tissues from the box and tried to use them put out the fire in the trash basket. That didn't go well. We grabbed more paper, this time just regular paper off the shelf and started fanning the flame. Yeah, bad idea. In the end, we found some random drink in a mug, probably coffee, and poured it in the trash. It all happened rather quickly, but boy was it exciting. Next, we piled more scrap paper and tissue on top to cover the wet things at the bottom. Suddenly, Mrs. Hills walked in. She paused, looked around in the air, looked at the desk and trash bin, then sat down at her desk. She never said anything, but I had a feeling that she knew we had done something. She kept looking up at Pam and me. It would be years before I would ever share that story.

During my middle school years, some kids at school accused my friend Pam and I of doing something wrong. I don't even remember what it was, but they told Mrs. Hills. The kids wanted us to get in trouble for whatever it was. You know how it can be at a small Christian school. Anything can seem big to kids there. Mrs. Hills could see that the other students in our group wanted us to have a serious punishment. She told them she'd take care of the situation. She called Pam and me in her office and told us to have a seat on the couch. Pam was sometimes defiant in stressful situations and refused to sit down. I think Pam was annoyed by the tattlers. Mrs. Hills didn't mind Pam's response. She just smiled and said that standing was fine. Then Pam sat on the floor. I sat on the couch. Mrs. Hills just sat at her desk for a few minutes working. Then she got up, told me to scoot over, and she proceeded to spank the arm of the couch. Pam and I took the cue. We gave our best yells and ouch sounds. This was one of my favorite trips to the principal's office during my whole middle school career.

One of the farthest shopping trips I went on with Mrs. Hills was to pick up workbooks for our school in a neighboring city. This trip took the whole school day, and I got to spend it with her. It was just Mrs. Hills and me. I shall never forget what a wonderful drive we had. She is quite the songbird, and we sang most of the way there. She shared stories about her dad, her mom, and growing up. On the way back to school, I felt a little sad that our time was coming to an end. On the other hand, I was so happy that she had chosen me for that trip. It lives in my memory as one the best school errands ever. When I think of the way Mrs. Hills made me feel when we were together, I know that God sees me even more so that way. I am His one and only. Yes, I understand God loves everyone. Nevertheless, I really feel like I am His one and only. I know that even when people wish me harm, God is merciful to me. The love He shows me every day is greater than any guilt, shame, or punishment someone thinks I deserve. He takes me on unique journeys and includes me in amazing plans. I am grateful that I had ten years of Mr. and Mrs. Hills loving me with the kind of love that God has for me. It has made all the difference.

Dolls and Fancy Cars

"I pray that He will give light to the eyes of
your hearts, so that you will understand the
hope to which He has called you, what rich
glories there are in the inheritance He has
promised His people, and how surpassingly
great is His power working in us who trust
Him. It works with the same mighty strength
He used." (Ephesians 1:18-19, CJB)

The dream life, as portrayed by a famous plastic girl doll with lots
of accessories, was one that many girls have desired growing up. The
endless wardrobe, the ability to do anything, have a job anywhere in
the world, and somehow still maintain a relationship with the acces-
sory boy doll that was her lifelong man appealed to me. This plastic
diva could position her plastic boyfriend anywhere she needed him
to be in her life. I loved my dolls. I had a lot of them, and I had just as
many accessories for them. I would say that my favorite imaginative
play of any of my toys was with these plastic dolls, and that's saying
a lot, because I had a ton of toys. Did you know my nickname until
the end of middle school was Barbie? That's what my teachers and
friends called me. My mom was a professional playtime imagineer.
She had the best storylines to go with the activity of my dolls of anyone I knew, and it wasn't out the question to have a few toy cars in on
the mix. She told the future with dolls and their fancy cars.

My mom loved to bring in a marriage scenario into our doll
play. She had everything planned out: the pre-wedding dinner, the
wedding rehearsal, walking down in a large stadium to meet the soon
to be husband, and of course, the awesome jobs these plastic diva

dolls had. Her grand doll house, with all her amazing furniture, was always placed so that there was plenty of space for the little dogs and tiny baby I used from another toy set. Yes, we mixed toys from other play sets into our doll dream house adventures. I loved this kind of time with my mom on so many levels. She had a rhythm in how the stories developed and was constantly casting a vision to me of my future. She was continuously pushing a narrative where these dolls were happily married, happily employed, and happily parenting happy children. My mom also frequently had my dolls be as diverse as possible. My mom was a community missionary for many years. I think she really sought to project a world to me where people from different ethnic backgrounds came together and worshiped, worked, played, married, and raised families. She was very strategic in her story lines. She always had a girl doll from one background marry a boy doll from a different one. She kept the adventures big. The dolls traveled far on mission trips, worked at their local churches, and held jobs that allowed them to serve others. My mom, without me realizing, was painting a picture of the world that she believed was my future. She was calling me out of my circumstances by faith and into what she believed was the life that my heavenly Father had waiting for me.

Serving is what my mom has done her whole life. Whether it's volunteering for VBS (vacation bible school), hosting a mission's night, or passing out food baskets, she has always been on the move for God. She knew her own marriage was full of woe. However, she really sought to see me in a better future. One of my favorite times playing is when I told her I wanted a fancy car when I grew up. In fact, I wanted a famous sports car that had come out in early 80's. She grabbed some toy cars from the toy box, and we pretended I had a car garage full of fancy cars. After we finished playing, she said to me seriously, "You can have a fancy car if you really want. You just have to work hard and ask God to help you make wise choices." As I got older, I changed my mind about wanting that car, but the message I received from my mom that day stayed with me. My life is not just what has been handed to me, it's what I invest in it that helps to shape my outcomes.

We can't change the circumstances we are born into, but we can choose the vision we believe for our future. My mom, for years through plastic dolls and fancy cars, cast a vision of my life and what I could and would do that was far bigger than the life I was living in as a child. My mother knew that I was more than what I was born into. She knew that God had better and bigger plans for me than what the enemy was constantly trying to get me to embrace. Today, I live out so much of what my mom role-played with me during my doll days. I believe that everything she said during our play time was intentional, and full of seeds of hope. Everyone can find a way to help others in dark and distressing places to see beyond where they are. Everyone can point people to hope, to Jesus. You don't need plastic and fashionable dolls or fast, stylish cars to do it. You can convey faith in so many ways. The word of God encourages us to be light in dark places, to offer a vision of promise to the hopeless. Let Holy Spirit teach you how to cast visions of hope to others in your sphere of influence.

Play a Game

"Each of you should use whatever gift
you have received to serve others, as
faithful stewards of God's grace in its
various forms." (1 Peter 4:10, NIV)

Video games have come a long way in my lifetime. I can remember the days when my family had to rent a movie and video player from a store to watch a movie. Thus, you won't be surprised that my early video games involved a dot bouncing back and forth from a thick line on each side of the screen. My parents appreciated technology in general, and my dad tried to keep up as best as our finances would allow. We had the expanded cable package. We ultimately purchased our own video player and recorder. Eventually, my parents conceded and gave me a popular game system. It was a time to rejoice. I had never had an official game system before. It was time to play a game.

Around this same time, my cousin Manny was needing a place to stay while he was in some sort of living transition. I really don't remember what brought him our direction. However, my mom was very excited to host him at our home. My dad, who was in his hardcore years of abusing me, lightened up on his debauchery when my cousin arrived. My father did his best to be a semi-normal parent, and I prayed that Manny would stay a long, long time. Manny was an artist. He still is. I can remember looking at one of the paintings he had brought to our house. It was amazing. I was in elementary school at that time, but I remember most of the time I had with Manny.

Manny had his business and activities in Houston, but at the end of his busy day, he would invite me to sit on the floor in our family room and play a game. He and I must have played on my game system almost every night he was there. I cherished every minute of it. While I played, I would imagine that sitting with a guy like him and just having a fun time was normal. Manny made it feel normal. He made me believe that the good times we were having, without me needing to give back to him in some physical way, could be a standard way of living. There I was just hanging out with a guy, in the intimacy of my home, and having fun! I let those memories burn in my soul. Those remembrances carried me in some of the tough moments of renewing my thought life over the next several years. I must have shared about Manny and how he played on that game system with me in some of the most traumatic years of my life with many people before I finally got an opportunity to tell him.

Life is difficult, but life is good. Those who step out of their own difficulty and share goodness and love with others are the ones that come to realize something very important. No matter how difficult life is, you can be the good. You don't have to do great things to change the world, just do something. One little something at a time to affect change in one life: a smile to someone looking sad, or a hello to someone who seems lonely, pausing an extra minute or two to carry on a conversation and listen to a stranger who just needs a friendly ear, taking the time to brighten up a child's life by spending time with them in play. These are the bricks that pave the road for God's love to travel on. What Manny had done, gave support to me that was deep during my childhood years and has stayed with me my whole life. Never underestimate the power of simply taking the time to sit and play with a child or any other seemingly simplistic God-centered act of love. You could leave a blessing that lasts a lifetime.

Forgotten Daughter

"But you are a tower of refuge to the poor,
O Lord, a tower of refuge to the needy in
distress. You are a refuge from the storm and
a shelter from the heat. For the oppressive
acts of ruthless people are like a storm beating
against a wall..." (Isaiah 25:4, NLT)

I have a sister. She is older than me and from a previous relationship my dad had before he met my mother. My father occasionally had my sister around me when I was too young to remember. However, by the time I got old enough to know who my family was, I had no idea she existed anymore. No one ever talked about her, at least not around me. From my "little girl" worldview at that time, my sister was a well-kept secret, until one day after my mom picked me up from my Christian school. My parents sat me down in the family room while my dad explained to us that we had a sister and that she was coming to visit with us. Then they sent me to my room while he and my mom talked. I had a feeling this was a rather sudden and unexpected life change for my mom as well.

As I sat in my room, I was so confused. How did I have a sister? I wasn't mad about it, I just didn't understand what was really going on. I felt the emotions in the air between my parents. I sensed that my world was about to change. I had so many questions. Was my mom her mom? Was my dad her dad? How old was she? How come I never saw any pictures of her around our house? Eventually, my mom came to my room and I asked her these questions. She explained them to me as best she could. But, in a rather scattered and quick way. My mom explained to me that we had met before and that my sister used to come visit our house when I was little. I wondered, if my parents ever divorced would my dad forget about me like he did her? Part of me wished that would happen, while part of me felt sick inside at the thought. I had no idea what having an older sister meant, as I had been the oldest in my family until that point. I was to find out soon however, that she was already traveling our way and would be arriving soon.

When I met my sister, I felt weird. It was strange being related to someone so closely and not knowing them at all. She arrived wearing pants and dressed like average American girls dressed in the 80's. My church didn't believe women should wear pants. Therefore, the first change that happened for my sister was her wardrobe. My father took her to the store to pick "appropriate" clothing. Next, my father cleared out my toy room to make a bedroom for her. I was upset by this. Little did I know how much suffering she would endure in that room with my dad.

I had a lot of different emotions pouring through me at this time, jealousy being right at the top. It was little things that my dad did for her that bothered me. My dad took her to pick what furniture she wanted for her room. She chose a canopy bed. I had always wanted one myself, so I felt very jealous about that. My sister had her room decorated with splashes of pink and beautiful colors. I had wanted to do something in my room like that also. I felt annoyed that she was getting things I wanted. I talked to my mom about it. My mother told me that my dad hadn't seen my sister in a long time and that he was taking time to do special things for her. I've since asked Jesus to forgive me for such jealousy. Under normal circumstances, I should have celebrated her joys and blessings. But the reality was, she wasn't getting blessed. She was being bought off.

My sister told me that she was thirteen years old. She had curly hair, was tall, and she walked the way I walked. I had never met another girl who walked like me before. I thought she was beautiful. She had a beautiful smile. I loved to see her smile. She had dimples. We didn't talk much. My dad kept us apart mostly. He started taking her out places alone all the time. They would go to city events, shows, and other outings that he didn't want to include the rest of us in. When I would ask my mom why we couldn't go, she would say that she didn't want to go anyway. I began to feel jealous again about not being able to do all the seemingly fun things with them. I would lay in my bed and pout about it sometimes while I talked to God about how I felt. My dad and my sister increasingly did more and more things separate from the rest of my family. Even home activities we started doing separately. My mom and I would stay upstairs sometimes while he and my sister stayed downstairs to watch movies together. I really didn't understand why I couldn't go with them. It almost felt like we had two different families in our home.

One night, I asked my mom why I couldn't watch the movie with them. She told me I probably wouldn't like the movie. She didn't want me to go down there with them. I cried and made such a fuss until my dad said I could come. It was against my mother's best judgement. However, I crept slowly downstairs and tiptoed to the family room. My father didn't notice me come down at first. When I peeked into the room, I saw on the T.V. a boy walking into a room. I stood there long enough to figure out the boy was walking into the room of his little sister. I slipped into the room and sat on the floor. The movie made it clear the boy was related to the girl. Then the boy started to rape his sister. You would think this would have triggered something in me to run away quickly, but it didn't. I had never seen anything that seemed so familiar on T.V. like that, even how the girl just kept quiet about it. My dad had me move to the couch with him and my sister to watch the movie. He sat on the couch hugging my sister while I sat on the other side. I felt sick inside watching that movie with them. Eventually, I went to my room. I decided in my heart that I didn't want to watch any more movies with them. It was a little too much for me. My mom heard me come up and asked me about the movie. I tried to describe to her what I had seen. I could see my mom's face looked really concerned. As soon as my dad went to my parent's bedroom late that night, I heard my mom fussing at my dad.

I'm not sure how long my sister visited with us. However, the whole time she was there, my dad never did anything to me. He had stopped coming into my bedroom at night entirely while she was there. I remember that very clearly. I began to get used to him just hanging out in my sisters' room and, though I had an idea of what might be going on, I really didn't understand it was wrong completely. You know that feeling you have when you know something is not right, but you feel like your estimate of the wrongness of it may not be correct? That's how I felt. No one in my home had any clear conversations with me about what abuse was at that time. My mom talked about it, but she used words that were coded from my perspective. I'm certain she believed I understood. I didn't. Therefore, it hadn't registered in my head that I could help my sister and myself by talking to my sister honestly. We could've put our stories together to get free maybe. None of that was on my radar. Looking back on those years, I'm saddened that I never got to know her well when she lived with us. It breaks my heart.

I came home one day from school and my sister was gone. My mom and dad were very upset. My mom was crying and my dad stayed in his room raising his voice. He was clearly angry. I asked my mom what was going on with my dad because he seemed extra mean and emotional after my sister left. My mom told me not to worry about it. Years later I found out that my sister had tried to file charges against my father for all he had done to her. As it turns out, my dad really used her in some awful ways before he dumped her again. Through the years I didn't talk to my sister as much as I probably should have, but I really feel I understand her better than she probably realizes. When I think back on the patterns my dad had with my sister and the way he interacted with her, its exactly like he became with me as I got older. So, I don't have to think too hard about the journey she had staying with us. My father forgot my sister, again, as soon as she wasn't performing for him the way he wanted. He did the same to me when I found my strength and finally left for college. His exact words to me my senior year, which was the year he finally left me alone, was "I'm not paying for anything for you for your last year of high school or college." He was mad at me. When he dropped me off at college, my mom was trying to take notes on a piece of paper so she could remember how to get there. My father took several unnecessary exits and turns on purpose only to confuse my mom. Then when we arrived, he told me he wasn't ever going to come get me. With tears in her eyes my mom said she would come get me. To which my dad responded, "good luck getting here." Thus, I understood how my father just dumped my sister like an old rag once he decided he couldn't get anything else out of her.

My sister had some help from her mom and grandmother. However, she sank deep into despair and depression before she was able to come up for air. I love her so much. I regret that I didn't know what I know now. I feel like we could have helped each other. That was part of our dad's plan, to keep us apart and keep us from knowing each other's stories. I encourage anyone who has a story to tell to share it whenever Holy Spirit leads you to. Your story may help free someone else. It could become part of someone's healing journey. If I could go back in time to talk to my sister at the time of her deepest hurt, I would tell her this: "Sister, we may be forgotten daughters to our earthly father, but we are not forgotten by our heavenly Father. He loves us and wants to heal us completely. And I promise you this, He is nothing like our dad. He holds us with an everlasting love that is good, and safe. Jesus wants you to know that you were never alone and that His love is stronger than your pain. And I want you to know that you are not a forgotten sister. You are loved."

"But you belong to God, my dear children.
You have already won a victory over those
people, because the Spirit who lives in
you is greater than the spirit who lives
in the world." (1 John 4:4, NLT)

"I am the LORD, the God of all the
peoples of the world. Is anything too
hard for me?" (Jeremiah 32:27, NLT)

My Victory Torch

"Go to the people of all nations and make
them my disciples. Baptize them in the name
of the Father, the Son, and the Holy Spirit,
and teach them to do everything I have told
you. I will be with you always, even until the
end of the world." (Matthew 28:19-20, CEV)

Victory is not a word that comes to mind when you are living in pain. However, according to scripture, the victory is already ours through Jesus. Indeed, Victory is not just a word to be said at the end of a long battle, and its presence is not determined by the quantity or quality of scars thereafter. Those that believe such untruths sometimes die on the vine before their fruit is revealed. Victory is something I longed for as a child. I desperately wanted to know how to overcome my pain, guilt, shame, and all the dysfunctions I experienced. I prayed often for the ability to rise above those things. One day, the Lord spoke to me when I was young and unwrapped a beautiful truth. A triumphant life is embodied in a God who gave everything so we can live victoriously now, not at the end. This was something tangible that I was called to pass on.

Growing up in Texas, I can say that God put many people in my life that tried to help me visualize the path of a beautiful, victorious life. My momma being the first of those to do so, was always speaking a better picture of myself to me. But like other church babies in the world, the Word was so normal in my universe that many times I was hearing, yet not hearing. According to the scripture Shema, most recognized in the line "She-ma Yisrael" translated "Hear, O Israel" in Deuteronomy 6:5, "Hear" is a word of action and through hearing and doing we receive the blessings of the word of God. I was always told that if I follow God's word, I would be blessed and be able to overcome anything and have victory. I had many blessings, but could not see anything other than the abyss I was presently in. Not much victory was going on in those days in my home. When I heard "victory in any circumstance," I was only hearing it. I did not understand that I was responsible to act in faith on that word.

Don't get me wrong, some of my life's issues were clearly beyond my control. In that season of my life, any measure of victory seemed elusive and almost impossible. Some of the steering of my childhood's direction was not determined by me, but by those around me. It's a pretty helpless position to be in as a child when a key adult in your life is drunk at the wheel. Even in this, I experienced God's fire, flames of love that consumed my hopelessness, replaced it with hope and flung open the doors to intimacy with God. This allowed me to get sneak peeks into the overcoming life that I would have. This opening of my heart's eyes to doors of my victory was heightened in a seemingly insignificant moment in middle school.

The Christian school I went to in Texas had chapel on Wednesdays. Sometimes my principal would play the piano and we would all sing songs, and sometimes a guest speaker would come and share some tidbit with the students. It was always thought-provoking on some level and I looked forward to it each week. One Wednesday, the guest speaker was a friend's mom. My friend Nelly's parents had done some local missionary work and came often throughout the school year to speak. On this day, Nelly's mom shared on Matthew 28:19-20. In addition, she shared a song with us. It was called "Pass it On", a song by Kurt Kaiser written in 1969. She sang all three verses. Her mom had a lovely voice, and many of my friends sang along. I chose not to sing along, because I was captivated by the words, what the words necessitated, and the gifts that were to be had thereafter by living out what the song said. The lyrics painted a heavenly reality of life that I wasn't experiencing. When I heard this song, I heard how to begin living a victorious life. This life would not depend on the circumstances of my existence, but only on the choices I made. During the last verse, it was as though I was being invited to join in this "flowers blooming, bird singing, flames of love" burning life. I felt like it was God making it very clear that my victory was His. He had done it, and He wanted me to have it regardless of what ship or waves I was riding.

When I went home that day, I was determined to live above my trauma. I began thinking more about the fire of God, Holy Spirit living in me. I was around people all the time, but did I radiate the love of who He is to others? Or, was that love blocked by my own pain, causing me to be more self-focused on my own issues and needs? Afterall, my messed-up life wasn't my fault, so how much was I accountable for? And yet, the words of the song suggest I was accountable to pass something on.

What was that something? It was Yeshua, honest and true. Not the look good on the outside but falling apart on the inside perspective of Christ I had been living. I wanted to move into a real, open, and honest life, where genuine overcoming happens, where Jesus happens and changes everything. Jesus was more than my best friend. He is God, the embodiment of God's victory for humankind. Yes, I was in a battle of insurmountable measure, and I was to stay in that battle for many more years, but I no longer wanted to live in pause mode, waiting for the end to come before I began to experience victory. I began to realize that my scars didn't diminish the victory I had already through the living and present love of Christ in my life. I began to renew my mind with Bible truths like Philippians 4:13, Psalm 139:14, John 8:36 and Psalm 23:6. I also started to become more aware of the how Holy Spirit was moving in those around me. I started seeing amazing things God was doing in others. My faith began to grow. My sense of who I was, and what I was capable of in Jesus, began to grow. I began to see God's heart for me more clearly. I was still a long way from freedom. However, a boldness began to develop in me. I began to pray more for others who were on their own ships of pain and despair. I found supernatural courage to pray and believe seemingly impossible things with others.

Looking back on this time of my life, I am aware that as I stepped into faith for others and their healing, I was able to see beyond my circumstances into hope. Before that time, hope seemed only like a churchy word with no basis in reality. As my mind began to transform, so did my perspectives about the people, places, and circumstances I lived in. I began to feel less and less overcome by my pain and more able to overcome the guilt and shame that entered my mind. I still carried the heavy weight of what I was living through. However, I realized I was beginning to live in the victory I now knew was mine and started taking small, yet bold, steps in a direction of freedom, and it was all because of God and power of His Word.

It was also around this time that I knew what I was to do with my life. When I was much younger, I felt a call to missions. I believed that one day God would send me out both far and near to sow seeds for the Kingdom. When I had been younger, I dreamed of becoming a doctor, becoming a Nun, and marrying Luke from the famous television town of Hazard County. Now that I was in middle school, I understood that becoming a nun and marrying Luke were not exactly compatible. However, I knew with absolute clarity that my calling was to spend the rest of my life leading others to the deep well of God's triumphant love. I didn't know if it would be by becoming a doctor, but I knew whatever skills God gave me, I would use for what He was calling me to. I was getting a taste of that depth of His heart for me and felt honored to surrender my life to this kind of love. Without Him, I would have been destroyed. While I was a sinner, He died for me. He paid the price so I can have victory now. Jesus is the captain of my ship and, as long as I live, I will continue to "Shema" a little better each day, allowing the fire of His Holy Spirit to point others towards Truth. I accept the mandate to love boldly, see the beauty of God in those He created, trust that His goodness and mercy is forever, and point others to Jesus through whom we have our victory. I want to pass the victory torch on.

"Surely goodness and mercy shall follow me
all the days of my life: and I will dwell in the
house of the Lord forever." (Psalm 23:6, KJV)

BROKEN

My Future Husband

"The LORD is near to all who call on him,
to all who call on him in truth. He fulfills the
desires of those who fear him; he hears their
cry and saves them." (Psalm 145:18-19, NIV)

A few weeks into tenth grade, my family moved to a different neighborhood, which put me in a different school district. We had moved to Washington state before I entered ninth grade previously. Up to this point, we had only been living in Washington for close to two years. I had already moved twice and attended two high schools for ninth grade. I was unsettled by another move. I found public school to be profoundly different than the Christian school I had come from. It lacked the type of Christian community I had been used to. It didn't feel safe, and I was bullied often for how I dressed, my Texan accent, and for my love for Jesus. On top of that, my home life was a wreck. With all that going on, I was excited for the opportunity of a do-over during my sophomore year. What I didn't expect was just how distinctive the year was to be. That was to be the year I met my knight.

At our new home, some of our neighbors were believers in Jesus. My mom and I began to build relationships with them. One of those neighbors, Kathleen, was a senior at the new high school I was attending. On my first day at the new school on the way to the bus stop, Kathleen invited me to join her at the weekly prayer group that met at our high school before classes began. She had recently lost her mother to cancer and this group was very important to her. I said yes and was excited to connect with other believers on campus. When we arrived, the leader of the prayer group was playing some songs on his guitar. Next to him, stood a boy with dark brown hair, blue eyes, and the cutest smile I'd ever come across. He wore a white t-shirt, dress slacks, and black and white converse hi-tops. He was beautiful! I couldn't take my eyes off him. When we got to our prayer time, while everyone had their eyes closed and heads bowed, I kept taking peeks at him. I had never had a response like that to a guy before. My heart skipped all kinds of beats. I was raptured, and there was no going back.

After the prayer group, I found my way to my new classes. I was happy to discover that beautiful boy in my Spanish class. I sat in the seat I was given and thought how neat it was that we were in the same class. As the days went by, I found the courage to ask him his name. He said it was Paul. Kathleen, who invited me to the prayer group was Paul's secret pal. We all had "secret pals" in our prayer group. Her job was to pray for him and slip notes of encouragement and scriptures into his locker. She told me that since it was her senior year, she had a lot to do and asked if I would take that job over for her. I was ecstatic to do so.

I also told my mom how amazing Paul was. She told me to ask him what his goals were in life. At my mother's request, I did. Paul told me he believed God was calling him to missions and outreach. Though he wasn't sure what that would look like when he was older, he had already started making plans to go on his first major mission trip. He hoped to someday have a wife and kids as well. Since he wanted to spend as much time with his family as possible, he planned to work at a nearby gas station so he could see them often. My soul soaked that up like a sponge. That's exactly what I wanted: a man who loved God and loved his family. I went home and told my mom. She wasn't as excited as I was about his goals at the time. On the other hand, fast forward 10 years later, she was the one who made me call him to go out on our first official date. So, he obviously grew on her.

As the weeks went on, Paul became very excited to see me. In class we started sitting next to each other and we would talk about life, church, the Bible, and music. I really wanted his phone number, so I came up with an idea. My mom liked to shop at the dollar store, and on one of those trips I purchased a phone book. I brought it to Spanish class the next day and told Paul that I had a new pocket phone book. I told him that it didn't have any contacts in it, and I was hoping he could help me by putting his contact information in it. That made sense to him, so he gladly put his full name address and phone number in my book. Jackpot! I could call him now! And call him I did, though, not right away. I just held onto the information for several weeks. Eventually, I needed to call him.

I needed to call somebody. My mom had something going on in this season of her life, I can't recall what it was, but it kept her from being home when I got back from school. At those times, it was only my dad and me at home. That was a very perilous situation to be in. I lived in fear during that hour or so while my mom and brothers were gone. My dad got bold and began to try and force himself on me during those times. I had become pretty vicious. I fought and clawed with my long nails. I practiced what I later found out were fairly close to Jiu-Jitsu moves by getting him on the ground and twisting my legs, stopping him from making certain moves on me. It was a stressful time for a tenth grader in high school. One day out the blue, as I was walking in the door, I heard my dad coming out of his room. I decided to call a friend. I ran to the phone and dialed Paul's number. I had, of course, memorized it by this point having looked at it so many times in my phone book. His family answered. I asked to speak to him, and they gave him the phone. He was a man of few words, but I chatted and chatted and didn't stop until my mom got home. My dad, I found, was too afraid to "mess with" me and too afraid to unplug the phone lest the person I was talking to would assume something was wrong. In my family background, "mess with" was the phrase everyone used to describe being sexually assaulted by someone else. My dad would tell me to get off the phone, but I stayed on until my momma came home.

This became a regular routine for Paul and me for the next three years. After my sophomore year, I moved again back into the previous public school district. Paul was going to drop out of school, so his parents signed him up for a Christian school in town. Even though we only saw each other twice in our total high school years after that, Paul stayed a true and faithful friend. Whenever I came home to just my dad, I would go straight for the phone, call Paul and just talk about anything and everything until my mom came back. Paul would talk some, but mostly let me talk. He never told me he had to leave or get off the phone. He would take the phone with him to eat when his family was eating. He would put me on hold if he had to go to the bathroom, but would come right back. He was patient and kind with his words. He would pray for what I asked him to pray for. And even though I never told him what was going on in my home, I believe that his spirit could discern it. He responded to calls as though they were emergencies and he lightened my stress and burdens during those times with his funny ideas and interesting stories. He had a way of making me feel as though there was no one more important to talk to but me. I loved him. I really did. Long before thoughts of marriage or dating ever entered my heart, I loved him.

Paul protected me so many times throughout my high school years without even knowing it. His love for God and faithfulness to the word of God left a deep impression upon my life. During my senior year, as I was preparing for graduation, I saved up my money to buy a class ring. It was black gold and had leaves on it. I chose to put Paul's birthstone in it, but not because I thought I would end up marrying him. In truth, I didn't think it was possible, as I figured that lots of girls would snag him up quickly. I wasn't at a place in my life to even be able to process a relationship with anyone. I knew it too. I just wanted Paul's birthstone in my ring so that I could always be reminded of him and the type of character and care I wanted from a future husband. I didn't want myself to ever get sidetracked into something less than what I discovered was the best. He was my knight, protecting me, fighting off the despair and abuse one phone call at a time. What a beautiful man he is. I love him. I really do.

"God Kept releasing a flow of
extraordinary miracles through the
hands of Paul." (Acts 19:11, TPT)

The Great Hamster Chase

"What the Messiah has freed us for is
freedom! Therefore, stand firm, and
don't let yourselves be tied up again to a
yoke of slavery." (Galatians 5:1, CJB)

In high school, my family raised hamsters. They were very thera-
peutic, and I enjoyed them very much. My dad wasn't fond of them.
Nevertheless, my mom was very creative in helping us to get and
keep them. We had to do lots of things in an innovative way living
with my dad. He abhorred anything that brought joy to our home,
unless it was for him. Mom had to be resourceful when it came to
us having fun. When my dad was away on an Army Reserves trip,
she put together a party and a slumber party that night for me. For
the party, she also secretly purchased a used waterbed from a garage
sale down the street. I had always wanted a waterbed. My mom went
all out for me. There was an abundance of food, balloons from the
dollar store, Christian music videos, and dancing. We even took the
hamsters out to play with us.

As it turns out, the hamsters enjoyed their newfound freedom
and decided to explore that freedom a bit further. My mom, brothers, and I then embarked on "The Great Hamster Chase." Some people at the party helped in the search. We interpreted our hamster's
behavior of going on the run as them getting lost. Though looking
back on it, I think they weren't getting lost, they were finding out
how they were really created to live. Free.

My relationship with my dad was very different at that time of
my life than it was as a younger child. I had become somewhat more
aware of the unhealthiness in my family. And ever since ninth grade,

I began to fight back whenever he made attempts to force himself on me. I even started sleeping with one of our big kitchen knives in case he came into my bedroom at night. To further set boundaries, I would let him know that I would keep one eye watching for him and would kill him or die trying. This began a sleep deprivation issue that continued years into my marriage, because I had developed such strange night habits to protect myself. This began to limit the extent of what he could do to me. I had let my nails grow very long. I have strong nails, and they were great for short-term protection. Mind you, it would seem to most that calling the police was in order. However, if you've ever grown up in domestic abuse, you understand when I say that people trapped in a box of violence with walls on every side really can't visualize the outside of the box very well. And, when you can't visualize the outside of your abuse, sometimes it doesn't occur to you to call the police or tell someone. This is especially true when all the people you know are also trapped in the same box.

I needed to talk to someone outside of my family circumstances, someone who had not been conditioned toward abusive behavior towards them. I did have some people like that in my life. One of them was Paul, who I ended up marrying years later. At the time, I didn't even perceive that I could talk to him about that. This was not because of him, but my own poor insight into what life was like beyond what I had become used to.

My dad was the lead pastor of my childhood church through eighth grade. We were always interacting with lots of other families who had a wide range of lifestyles and family issues. If you've ever been a P.K. (preacher's kid) then you understand. Even though I'm sure as pastors my parents encountered all kinds of situations in their counseling of others, there never seemed to be anyone to help us. I think all pastors need a pastor or trustworthy team they can go to when trouble and temptations arise. The truth is, I had no certainty in my head that I was being abused until I took a sex education class at my public high school my freshman year. Even then, I questioned in my thoughts if it was really abuse since my dad was so respected, and everyone liked him. It's not that my mom didn't talk about good touches or bad touches when I was growing up. In part, it's how she explained it. She was always trying to be careful about her words and hedged a few so that they weren't too strong or bold. She would always say that neither she nor my dad would do anything to hurt me. This is very confusing when you are a little kid and being abused. I was confused about what was okay and not okay in my home or even outside of my home.

During my freshman year, my dad was put on the ministry team at a church in Washington. Around this time, my dad would beat me profusely if he thought I was 'telling our business' outside of my home. I was so confused, even as a ninth grader. I was convinced that anyone who knew my dad would say I was a liar if I told the breadth of what was going on. And the few times I tested the security of my "cage" by telling my mom, friends, random cousins, strangers at school, or strangers in public places, nothing happened. Everything stayed the same. Honestly, I don't think anyone really knew what to say or do to help me. I think it must be scary for people to hear such things. Maybe they feel helpless in knowing how to help someone in those situations, even if they love them. I even wrote two letters to two different high-profile persons outlining everything and only got autographed pictures back. It sounds silly, but I truly thought I wouldn't be believed or heard. When you are in this kind of predicament, you become like a hamster in a cage. All your attempts to get free involve spinning in a wheel going nowhere. You feel alone, always looking outside of the cage but never really knowing how to get out.

However, you really aren't as trapped as you think. It's just that all the ways that "they" on the outside of your situation say works to get out doesn't always work for you. In theory, they should, but then there is reality. For me, God had to use people way out of my normal world to help me to even understand what I was living in before I could start to see life differently. Every cage has its own design and the locks and exits are all unique. My cage of fear didn't have the most obvious exit to me. I struggled most of my high school years with how to protect myself, how to help protect my mom, and how to reduce the situational violence towards my brothers. In addition to this, I spent a lot of time imagining how to get free.

When I was in high school, my grandmother came to visit us. She lived over 2,000 miles away down in Houston and had never flown on a plane. She was born near the end of World War 1, and my brothers and I were some of her younger grandchildren from her younger children. Due to her apprehension of planes, she took a bus with one of my besties, Christie Love, who is also my cousin. I was super excited about seeing both of them, and my mom and I made all kinds of plans for their arrival. Unfortunately, my grandmother, who was beginning to show signs of Alzheimer's, emotionally and mentally fell apart going through the mountainous regions during the trip. The bus driver had to release my grandmother off of the bus. They were still several hours away, having to sleep in a shelter.

Oh, it was stressful for my mom and all her siblings who lived far away. My mom asked my dad to drive and go get my grandmother and cousin. He said no. However, two of my uncles started driving from thousands of miles away to get her. I believe my dad felt shamed into it, and therefore he reversed his answer to a yes. My mom, not trusting my dad, asked if I would ride with him. Because I loved my grandmother, I went. However, I was terrified. An eight to nine-hour drive with my dad alone had nightmare written all over it. I sucked up my fear and stepped into his truck.

I sat as close to the passenger door as possible. Eventually, we arrived to where my grandma and cousin were at night. The place where my grandmother and Christie Love were staying was a free women's shelter and locked their doors after a certain hour. We wouldn't be able to get them until the next morning. My dad decided to park in a closed mall parking lot to wait out the night. That's when the evening horrors began. I fought and screamed and eventually I reached the handle of the passenger door and screamed outside. He told me to stop screaming. I could see he was afraid at this point. I told him I was going sleep outside and if he touched me again, I would scream as loud as could. He begged and pleaded with me to stop. Eventually, I did stop screaming.

I stayed up all night long in case he changed his mind about leaving me alone. It was a very traumatic and tiring night. The next morning, I was so very tired. I literally had not slept in two days for fear of being raped and spent a good amount of that time fighting. After picking up my grandmother and cousin, my dad bought cinnamon rolls for us to eat for breakfast. He acted as though nothing had happened the night before. I learned two things during this trip. One, my cousin doesn't like icing on her cinnamon rolls. Who knew! The other, is that my dad was afraid of being known by people outside of his inner circle. This was a major weak spot in the cage he thought he had us trapped in.

On another occasion a few years later when I was sixteen, my dad was teaching me to drive. I didn't want to learn to drive. My mom had come from a family where it took many years for some of her older family members to learn how to drive. Since it was my senior year, she insisted that I learn before I graduated. My mom would stay home with my brothers sometimes, and I would have to go out with my dad alone. It was always a traumatic experience. He was constantly putting his hands up my dress while I was trying to drive, forcing his tongue into my mouth. The ladies in my family were only allowed to wear dresses or skirts. Baggy long shorts were okay as well. I personally still love my dresses for church. Then again, I will say that they were a horrendous choice of clothing when going out driving with my dad. I started wearing leggings under my dresses, even though the dresses were already super long. It didn't stop him, but it did give me some space to delay things.

One day while I was out driving with my dad, I had an epiphany! I realized that If I ran into a large tree at a very high speed, he could very well die. Sure, I might die as well, except at that point in my life I was fine with that trade. I knew where I was going. So as soon as I saw the first big tree in my view, I gunned the gas pedal straight towards it. It was, to say the least, exhilarating as thoughts of my mom's and brothers' freedom flashed in my mind. However, my dad was stronger and grabbed the wheel holding tight, pulling it away from the tree and back to the road. He left me alone on the way home that evening. My dad never took me out driving again. Maybe I scared him. I wasn't trying to scare him. I just wanted him removed from the earth so that my family could be free. That beautiful event gave me a surge of boldness from that day on that never left me. It didn't stop him from harming me, however he took a few steps back in the severity of it. It was occasions like that that allowed me to see other avenues of escape. I became like a hamster, trying to find the weak spots in my cage.

Through all this, my dad was persistent. He had a perverse sexual addiction. On one occasion, which I still think of when I am driving in that area of town, I realized just how deep my dad's struggles were. Near the end of my senior year of high school, I can't remember why, but for some reason I was sent to the store with my dad. We stopped at Safeway and got whatever we were sent to get. Then we got back into my dads' truck. Instead of driving back home, he started driving down towards the freeway. I asked him where we were going. He didn't say anything. I started to get really concerned and demanded he tell me where we were headed. He said in the most cheerful tone, "I am taking you to a hotel where we can spend time together for your graduation." My mind was blowing up over this comment. I had a flash back of all the terrible horrors I had already faced with him and realized that my only option was to jump out of the truck. So, I opened the passenger door while he was cruising down the highway. He yelled to me, "What are you doing!" I was thinking to myself, "You are doing crazy, I can do crazy too." I told him I was going to jump out of the truck. He begged and pleaded for me to stop, all the while pulling on my left arm. I told him If I die on the freeway then everyone would question what was going on and my mom and brothers would be free of him while he rotted in jail. He began to turn the truck around back towards home and when he did, I closed the door. The whole way home he begged and pleaded for me not to tell my mom. Of course, I told her. But as it was in those days of our lives, she was a victim as well and had been in an abusive relationship with my dad much longer than I had. A drowning person can't save another.

It rarely works out well to get help from another victim in your same situation or worse. You do have a certain amount of comfort at times knowing you're not alone in difficult things. However, so often they too are afraid and can't envision life outside of their own cage. Little did I recognize, but my mom did have a better vision for her future. At the time, however, she didn't know how to accomplish it. I will say this about my mom, I've learned a lot from that lady through the years. Her stability to my brothers and me and her total devotion to Christ are what kept us going during those years of abuse. No matter how discouraged and helpless I could feel in my efforts to talk to her in that season of our lives about the things going on with me, I knew there was no sense in holding her inability to help me against her. It did really hurt to feel like you can't get protection from the people that everyone says you should go to for protection. Hurt is an expected emotion under the circumstances. Even so, God has helped, even as a child, to see how much pain my mom was in. I knew her vault of traumas was every bit as big as mine. Holy Spirit has helped me through the years to recognize the need to give forgiveness, even in incomprehensible circumstances.

My family life didn't change much after what happened with my dad in town that day, except one really big thing did happen for me personally. That was the last time my dad ever touched me, which brings me back to the hamsters. Did we ever find the missing hamsters? Indeed we did, although not before spending the rest of the next day tracking them down by following a hamster poo trail. We found them all eventually. One hamster had found a new home inside the couch. I imagine the space was amazing for it. We didn't find the others until my dad returned from his trip. Before he returned, we partied hard. We played and ate, and jumped on my waterbed until it burst. It was a blast. A few hours before my dad's return, everyone left the party and went home. My mom, brothers, and I cleaned the wet floor in my bedroom and threw away the busted waterbed. As Mom used to always say, "hide the evidence" before Dad would come home from anywhere. By the time he arrived, everything was clean, mom had a meal prepared for him, all party favors disposed of. The remaining hamsters were still loose. My dad never knew it, but he lived in a house with hamsters roaming free for a while. Eventually, we found the last one in my parent's shower nibbling at the bottom of the shower curtain. The remainder of my senior year, I was like that hamster, roaming free and unafraid of the adventure ahead. My dad's chase was done. He knew he would never catch me again.

"All who are led by God's Spirit are God's sons and daughters. For you did not receive a spirit of slavery to bring you back again into fear; on the contrary, you received the Spirit, who makes us sons and daughters and by whose power we cry out, 'Abba!' (Dear Father)" (Galatians 5:1, CJB)

The Great Escape

"You, my brothers and sisters, were called
to be free. But do not use your freedom to
indulge the flesh; rather, serve one another
humbly in love." (Galatians 5:13, NIV)

The year I went to college was full of transitions. I chose to go to George Fox College, a small Christian Quaker school in Oregon. This turned out to be one of the best life choices I have ever made. So much of my healing ended up happening there. I had, up to that point, experienced sixteen years of verbal, physical, and sexual abuse at the hands of my father, who was my pastor for many of those years. This school provided Christ-centered support for me from all angles. I finally felt safe. Although my family and I were still very connected to my dad, going away to college in a different state was freeing for me. I really had no desire to be close to home. My mother and brothers were still living in that unfortunate situation. And though I had location freedom, I did not have emotional freedom. My heart was tied to my mom and brothers. How could I be at peace knowing they were still living in that kind of hell? I prayed for their deliverance, for a Great Escape. One day it came. My mom had some amazing friends and they really saw more than my mom saw about her own situation at that time. It helps to have friends who care about you to see things from outside of your circumstances. Some of those friends were bold enough to declare ideas to my mom about leaving my father. I know she wanted to leave, but how could she? God knew. God also knows how to move us into His divine direction in creative ways. Thus, I believe that He allowed my dad to make a series of decisions that began to really make leaving seem more attractive than staying.

One of the first things my dad did was move my family to a new house while I was in college. My mom decided not to sleep in the master bedroom with my dad, but chose to sleep in what was to be my bedroom. My dad also became much bolder about his fooling around with his female clients who he was "counseling." My father was doing counseling work at the time, if you want to call it that. All of this happened without my mom truly understanding everything that was being done behind her back. My father controlled the flow of mail and resources in our home. He kept many things locked in his safe and had the mail going to a P.O. box that my mom had no access to. The combination of all my dad's behavior had now reached its zenith. My mother knew her freedom was past due.

My mom spoke to me over the phone and told me what had been going on. She said that her friends were going to help her escape. And they did. They got her in a safe house, and she was protected for a time until my dad moved out of the house. Then my mom and my brothers moved back into the house. However, my mom couldn't pay the bills for the house. She had been a full-time homemaker for the last fifteen years. Thus, staying there was only temporary since she had to move out herself. To add to our family stress, she had to make sure my dad didn't get custody of my brothers. This was a scary thought for us, knowing how unstable and sexually unhealthy he was. My mom asked me if I would be willing to share my experiences of abuse from my dad with the police. I had uncertain feelings about this. Yes, I certainly wanted to tell the police, but this was the first time I felt like I had permission from my mom to do so. In fact, it was the first time I realized that my mom had understood any of the experiences I had shared with her through the years.

Initially, her request felt like she was suggesting that it was okay to sacrifice me for all those years, but it wasn't acceptable to put my brothers through unforeseen dangers. I thought about all the times my mom made me apologize to my dad for upsetting him when he couldn't have his way, or her always telling me, "Remember, he's your dad." And the times she made me go out with him to dinner and pay for it with my work money because he told her I upset him. Honestly, for years I simply felt like I was in Loony World where things could happen to me, and no one closest to me did anything but make me apologize for protecting myself. So, my initial emotion to this request was not a good one. I felt used.

But my heart told me that wasn't true. I knew it was in my power to help my family, and I wanted to. I had gained location freedom, and now it was in my power to help my brothers and mother to have the same freedom. I loved them too much not to help, but I prayed and asked God to forgive me for having such a poor initial emotional response to my mom's request. My heart told me that I had been praying for my mom to have a situation that would open her eyes to how trapped she really was. It was my moment to humbly serve my family in love. I realized that she wasn't trying to use me or my pain to her advantage. Instead, this was an answer to my prayers. God had creatively orchestrated the right circumstances to push my mom out of her own cage and to a place of desperateness for something better. She was in as much pain as I was in that home. I think half the things I told her as a child were too much for her system to handle in those days. I think she felt helpless and hopeless during those years. And now, she was trusting me to help her and my brothers, because she knew I loved them. She knew I loved her. She knew I had been praying for their Great Escape.

I am sorry that my mom had to face so much horror as a wife. All her hopes that her husband would follow God were burnt to a crisp. I am sorry that she was so trapped that she lived victimized for so many years. I am sorry that so much of our life was sacrificed for the possibility of my father's repentance. I am glad that she was so faithful to the union of marriage. I am grateful that she modeled kindness and forgiveness in the toughest times. I am grateful that she was hopeful when hope seemed lost. I am most grateful that she never stops trusting the goodness of God, even when evil is everywhere. What a powerful testimony that has been for me in my life. I am saddened that my dad missed all those opportunities, but I am so grateful that God brought my mother to the doorway of her escape. Today my mom is free. So many of those years she doesn't remember. I'm certain that some of what I have been writing about is probably in the "I don't remember much about that anymore" part of her mind, and that's okay with me. It's probably for the best. It's more than enough for me that she believes me and that she is happy to listen to me now.

My mom has communicated to me several times that she is sorry for not fully hearing me through those childhood years of my life. She acknowledges she was a completely different person then. And she was. I tell my husband that the mom my younger brother has is not the mom I had. The woman my younger brother calls mom is the boldest, bravest, strongest woman I know now. She would never let anyone do even one percent of what my father did to her or us now. It's a good thing. She is a wonderful protector of children today. When God frees us, we truly are free. And with that freedom comes a new flow of wisdom, strength, grace, and power from the Spirit of God. Today, my momma becomes a total grizzly bear on anybody who tampers with the safety or joy of the children she cares for. My mom has really gained a wealth of wisdom and growth through her years of learning from her journey. I think she should write a book someday. Today she is a teacher, a mentor, and an accountability partner for others. She has since been a mom and protector to several needy and disabled children. Most importantly, she is a passionate servant of Jesus. She's even a cancer survivor. She really is an amazing woman! A true overcomer. You can't live through what she's lived through and come out the other side so beautifully and full of the love of God the way she has without Jesus. I'm proud of my momma. She is leaving a beautiful legacy.

Once my mom made her great escape, she boldly went in a healthy direction and didn't look back. If you need a new beginning, take encouragement from my mom. Whether you are a victim like she was, or an abuser like my dad, there is healing and redemption for you. Addictions, sins of all kinds, it doesn't matter. Jesus is the answer for all these issues. His Spirit can give you the strength and direction you need to eradicate all things that pull you away from Him and His good life for you. Give Christ your weighty issues and share your story with trusted people who can help you find proper

Christian counseling. Find people who will give you the accountability you will need to come alive in the light and not die in the shadows. If my mom can overcome all she went through and move into positive, God-breathed streams of life, then you can too. Step out on faith and trust that God can carry you through your Great Escape.

"The people who walked in darkness have
seen a great light; Those who dwelt in the
land of the shadow of death, upon them
a light has shined." (Isaiah 9:2, NKJV)

Ministry of Friendship

"My command is this: Love each other as I
have loved you. Greater love has no one than
this: to lay down one's life for one's friends. You
are my friends if you do what I command. I
no longer call you servants, because a servant
does not know his master's business. Instead,
I have called you friends, for everything
that I learned from my Father I have made
known to you." (John 15:12-15, NIV)

The day my momma left my dad was a day of new beginnings. Not just for her, but for me as well. My mother, brothers, and I, over the next several months, would experience a wealth of generosity, compassion, and help like we had not experienced before. So many people stepped out of their spheres of comfort to help us in unique ways extending their time, connections, and resources to us. Even Paul and his family were part of the helping. This was a season where God truly revealed to us what the ministry of friendship really looks like.

On the morning my mom left, one of her beloved friends, a beautiful German woman who knew the value of generosity, coordinated to meet my mother and my brothers not far from their house. But, before my mom departed, she lived life in the house with my dad as normal so she wouldn't draw attention to things. I don't know if she told my brothers what she had planned in full yet. She cooked food, labeled it, and put it in the freezer. The night before she left, she slept lightly, waiting until the planned get-away moment. Then, my momma and my brothers took their few belongings and trekked down the road to be picked up by her friend. That friend had everything organized for my mom and brothers. She had found a secret housing location at no expense to my mom. She provided trust, a safe house, and compassion at one of the most transitional times of our lives. My mom didn't tell me that she had even left until later. When she did, I felt relieved. To this day, I am grateful to that friend. She built a bridge for my family to cross to get to the doorway of freedom. That faithful friend passed away during the writing of this book, but we continue to be blessed by her brave act of friendship. Actions of love always continue beyond the grave. What she did for my family was the ministry of friendship in action.

Later, on the same day my mom left, my dad called me at George Fox College. He inquired as to where my mom was. I honestly didn't know, and I told him so. He concluded on the phone that maybe she was headed in my direction to Oregon. I told him I didn't think so, but I was scared when I got off the phone. You have to understand my history with this man. He's the same one who pulled over on the freeway in the fast lane to drag me out of the car to punch me and bang my head on the pavement, just because he was mad at my three-year-old brother. This is the same one who, when I failed to answer the phone, would find where I was and punch me in the face. So, even though I was several hours away at that time, I still feared what he could do if I was alone with him. He hadn't come to my college since he dropped me off. I didn't want him coming there now. If he came, I figured he would probably try to get me somewhere alone and beat me, try to rape me, and perhaps accidentally kill me in his rage. I really wasn't sure. I figured it was all dependent on how angry and out of control he would be upon arrival.

Now that I am years removed from all of this, I truly believe that he was far more terrified than I was. I imagine he knew he was going to have big trouble coming down the pipeline, and I think he was far too petrified to show his face on my college campus. However, as someone who just turned 17, and had just left an abusive situation, I did what a person afraid would do. I went and talked to our campus pastor, Mr. Gregg Lamm, about what was going on. He was very compassionate and talked with campus security about keeping a look out to make sure my dad didn't come on the campus. The school informed my dorm. Our dorm leader decided that all the girls should stay close together with me that night. Therefore, everyone on my floor all slept in one room. I didn't even know everyone on the floor. However, there they were, supporting me in my time of crisis. My heart was deeply ministered to that night. Even when I think of it today, it touches me deeply.

I filed charges against my father for abuse shortly after my mom left. Mr. Lamm, our campus pastor, bought a plane ticket for me to get to my court date. He even helped me set up my first bank account. A short time later, God used my friends from my college again to help me get to and from the airport for my court dates in Washington. Not only did they help me with the logistics of flying to and from home for those events, but they provided the emotional support I desperately needed before leaving on those trips and upon returning from them. I really began to see myself differently through their eyes, not at all like I had become convinced I was by my circumstances. I had an abundance of lies that covered the true and real me. My friends were helping daily to uncover who I was in God simply by loving me through my pain and seeing the best in me when I felt at my worse. I cherish those days, and they mean more to me now than they did then. That season sealed my heart to some of those friends.

Paul and his dad also played a major role in helping my family during this transitional season. My mom and brothers were offered some temporary housing from an organization that helps women in crisis. My mom needed help moving. I was still at college in a different state, but I knew I could depend on Paul. I called him up and asked if he could help my mom move. He and his dad said yes, and they coordinated with my mom and her friend Sister Barker on where to meet. I think this might have been the first time my mom and Paul's dad ever met. Most of our friendship had been developed over the phone up to that point. Thus, I think it's wonderful how God allowed my mom and my future father-in-law to meet. There is no better way to get to know a person in a genuine way than to walk next to them in their trials. After the moving work was done, Sister Barker and my mom treated Paul and his dad to a bucket of fried chicken. Paul still speaks of that day today. He loved the company, and he says the chicken was delicious. I believe this helped my mom to really respect Paul and his family in a deeper way, even if all Paul wanted to do when he grew up was work at a gas station! After all, it was my mom that insisted I call Paul to ask him out on our unofficial first date six years later.

God used the ministry of friendship in so many areas of my family's life my freshman year of college. My roommate's family was so kind to me as well. They welcomed me into their home and treated me like their own daughter. I spent time with her at her home during special family events, and it gave me the opportunity to see the kind of family that I hoped to someday have. My Bible study group on campus was so loving and prayed with me through all my court proceedings. The wealth I found in the kind generosity and hospitality of those around me was such a healing thing for my heart, especially coming from all my years of being convinced that no one would listen or believe my story. God used this time, not only to bring healing seeds to my family, but to show us the Ministry of Friendship. Today, I do my best to follow God's call to extend friendship to others.

A pastor once said in one of his sermons that friendship is something we gift. No one can make us give it. We can't force it from others. It must be given freely. And it's a gift that God gives us. I have thought about this, and I know that God has truly blessed me through this gift. Therefore, I ask God every day to help me be a good friend to those He has placed in my life. Everyone and anyone can participate in the Ministry of Friendship.

Auntie's Listening Ear

"Be free from pride-filled opinions, for
they will only harm your cherished unity.
Don't allow self-promotion to hide in your
hearts, but in authentic humility put others
first and view others as more important
than yourselves. Abandon every display of
selfishness. Possess a greater concern for
what matters to others instead of your own
interests." (Philippians 2:3-4, TPT)

Everyone needs a listening ear at some point in their lives. That person for me growing up was my cousin Christie Love. If I want to bounce crazy life ideas off someone in a quick minute, I go to her. We've traveled the world together on and off the beaten path. So, Christie Love knows me very well. She's no nonsense and to the point. She is like a cocoa bean, tough on the outside but made of pure goodness. She's always been that way. She's an amazing mix of being very fun, but also very practical. I have vested countless hours talking with Christie Love, but when I was in college, my talking needs altered.

I had just left home for the first time and was processing the trauma I had lived through. Around that same time, I began counseling and my heart felt raw. I had so much on my mind. There was everything from recuperating from my years of abuse, to developing more independence as a young adult. In the same season, I was wrestling with an eating disorder where I would binge eat chocolate, and other things I didn't need, and then purge. I met one of my beloved friends on one of my eating-to-purge sessions. We are still wonderful friends today, and I'm glad to say that we are both healed from that. But at that time in my life, while in college, I was pursuing healing for many life issues. I was going through some serious depression also, but you probably could have guessed that. It was during one of these days in my life I decided to call my cousin Christie Love. She wasn't available that day. However, her mom was.

Her mom answered the phone, and I still really needed to talk to someone, so I just stayed on the phone with my auntie. My auntie asked how I was, and I'm not sure why, but I just started spilling my beans. I probably was far more honest than I'd ever been about how I was doing. She was so calm. She listened to me and reacted with such a peaceful tone that it made it feel safe to share. When I got off the phone, I felt lighter. I was talking about some very burdensome stuff. The nice thing was I was pretty sure my auntie could handle it. She's a tough cookie, and very sweet. My auntie somehow heard everything I said and made me feel like she not only believed me, but sympathized with me. I went to bed that night a little healthier than I was before. Sometimes I think people just need someone to hear them. They aren't wanting responses as much as a friend to hear. The Bible speaks about being a good listener. I didn't tell her everything I was processing, but somehow I knew I could. As the days, weeks, and years went by, I had many more evenings where I just needed a listening ear. Sometimes it was my cousin, but I found that sometimes I would call just to talk to my auntie. I knew that I could probably tell her anything, and she wouldn't freak out over it.

My auntie was exceptional at helping to grasp how my mom was processing her own wounds. When I would talk to her about my inability to communicate certain life traumas to my mom, she would put herself in my mom's shoes and articulate to me how my mom might have been feeling or emotionally managing the things I wanted to discuss with her. My auntie was always so kind to my mom with her words without ever invalidating what I wanted to convey. My auntie could have been a diplomat if she wanted. She naturally seeks out ways to bring unity and understanding to situations. I needed that in my college years. I had a lot of questions and, though my auntie didn't have all the answers to my life's questions at that time, she knew how to take the time to listen to me and allow me to feel heard and validated. My auntie was like a mother figure to me. I have a wonderful mom, and I love her very much. However, I was processing a lot of emotions about my years of living in my childhood home.

I was working on trying to recognize and appreciate who I was. I was seeking a deeper reality of God's perspective of who I was, learning how to sort all my emotions towards my dad and processing general hurt from the sixteen years before. It was a challenging time for me. As much as I loved my mom, she herself was going through her own journey of healing at that same time. We were all in counseling in my new fatherless family. I wanted to talk to someone that was outside of my camp of pain, someone who wasn't wounded from the same factors I was. Therefore, Christie Love and my auntie were there, just one phone call away. If I needed a bestie, I knew I could always call Christie Love. However, when I needed a mom voice on the other end of the line, I could always count on my auntie's listening ear. It is so important to have distinctive people that we can call on in our lives that can hear us in different ways and reach us in different ways.

Sometimes I would talk to my auntie about my dreams. Though some of my dreams were calm or even prophetic, for years almost all were terrifying nightmares. I would dream about various scenarios pulled from my past about being raped or assaulted or molested. It was awful going to sleep, and I hated it. I used to pray every night not to remember my dreams. However, I almost always do. I had continuing trauma even in my dream life. My auntie would pray for me and offer suggestions on what I could do. Even though she couldn't stop those horrific nightmares, just knowing she was listening and, actively trying to help me, made a huge difference in my life. I didn't feel alone. I think sometimes when people are hurting and they share their hurt, they understand that it can't be fixed by talking, but it still helps them not to feel alone and desperate.

Many years have passed for me since college. I don't exist in a state of trauma like I did when I was young. I have had trauma since, but it always passes. I know that when those times arise, and when seasons are going wonderful, I can always call my auntie. She always listens so well and without criticism. She is one of the humblest women I know. She is wise about many things, and she is my best friend's mom. Can't beat that! She listens and asks questions about what I am saying, seeking clarity about the topic. I've always liked that about her. It shows that she really does care about what's going on. It doesn't bother her at all to allow her heart to be moved by your situation. She will weep with you and rejoice with you. Paul and I both have come to appreciate her consistency through the years of being so present to lend a genuine listening ear. I regard my auntie as a second mother to me. Everyone needs an auntie like mine. When was the last time you stopped to be a listening ear to someone? It's never too late to start.

Straight Shooter Mary

"Love should always make us tell the truth.
Then we will grow in every way and be more
like Christ, the head." (Ephesians 4:15, CEV)

I love people who aren't afraid to speak truth even when it is uncomfortable truth. I surround myself with people who live genuine, unhidden lives. I find the realness of an honest relationship healing and refreshing. During my years of college, if I ever wanted to have a conversation and get some seriously honest feedback, I would call straight shooter Mary. There are a few things to know about her. She's going to give you a piece of her mind if you say things that are off base. She's a decent listener, but a better advice giver. She may not dwell on one topic for too long, but she has sharp discernment for finding and correcting wrong ways of thinking. Straight shooter Mary is the lady to talk to if you are looking to bounce your thinking off someone. If she doesn't know the answer to something, she doesn't pretend to. She simply says she doesn't know. I like that about her. She is not afraid to be honest. In college, I occasionally needed to have someone who had a perspective of me who was outside of my circle and was direct and forthright. Straight shooter Mary was my go-to person in college whenever I really wanted to have clear feedback about my thoughts.

One occasion that really stands out to me when Mary delivered some hard-hitting truths was during my junior year of college. I was feeling particularly down. All my friends were talking about the plans with their dads over the break. Those conversations just rehashed all my emotions about my own dead relationship with my dad. I didn't want to be near my dad ever again, and yet I felt the barrenness of being fatherless. This wasn't new to me. I felt fatherless most of my life. I felt a combination of fury toward my dad for still being alive and regret that I had no relationship with him. And I was irate at myself for feeling both those emotions. I became despondent and talked to some casual friends on campus about it. With the best intentions, they were telling me that my dad really loved me, but I just didn't know it. They told me this to make me feel better. I appreciated their kindness, but it made me feel worse. My dad was horrible. His showcase of love was so destructive. Yet, I took the counsel from the conversation and tried to cheer myself up with it. I ended up that evening in my room crying in my bed. I picked up the phone and called straight shooter Mary. Mary asked why I was so upset, and I told her all about it. Mary listened as I said to her, "I understood that my dad really loved me". She cut me off in the conversation and said in a rather authoritative voice, "Oh no! He did not love you. What he showed you is not what love is. He is a sick man who has no idea what love is, so how could he love you?" I was speechless, but her words freed me from being enslaved to the lie that because he was my dad, he loved me.

No one had ever said that to me about my dad. Even growing up, it was supposed to be a given that he loved me. Yet somehow hearing this from straight shooter Mary was like a large anvil shattering a glass ceiling. I felt so many emotions in that moment. I started sobbing. Straight shooter Mary just let me cry a bit. I also felt very angry. I told her I really wanted him to love me. She went on to explain to me that though my dad failed at loving me, God has never failed. She talked with me about the reality of being God's daughter and what that means for my life. She encouraged me not to view my dad as my real father, but God as my real Father, which was a truer reality. She said it was awful that my dad didn't know how to be a decent person, but it didn't ruin me. She reminded me that I shouldn't seek to be fathered by a man who didn't know how to father. She said, "You don't need a crazy dad. What you need is your Heavenly Father who wants to heal you." For the first time, I realized that my earthly dad really was sick. Not like the insult, "you're a sick man", but he didn't understand God's love for him and what it meant to love his wife and children. He needed help long before I was born and didn't receive it. It was the first time I could see my dad in a different light, as a patient needing the Great Physician. Talking to Mary also freed me to let go of feeling that crazy emotional allegiance to my dad. I realized that it was more than okay to just release him from the duties and titles associated with fatherhood. I didn't need him to fill my empty dad hole. I needed to focus on intimacy with my Father in Heaven.

It's funny how one phone conversation can change your life. Ever since that day in my junior year, I have rarely felt angry about my dad's inability to love me the way the Bible says he should have. It is clear to me now that he just didn't know how. How could he when he himself was so broken and wounded from his own undealt with past? Ever since that conversation with straight shooter Mary, I realized that it's okay to accept the truth that my dad's broken and damaging love was unfit for me. I don't have to pretend that he really meant something different, because he didn't. That one phone call freed me to seek the love of my true father, God, on a much deeper level. I started to become more aware of His goodness and mercy in my life every day. I became so much healthier through the years the closer I got to God. I feel His love, His bold and safe arms around me all the time. I am so grateful that straight shooter Mary was painfully honest that day in college. It freed me to know the real love of my true Father. Have you ever felt prompted by Holy Spirit to speak truth to someone who has embraced something false? If God is leading you to do so, He will show you how to share that truth the way He wants it shared. Don't be afraid to speak truth. It could change the direction of someone's life.

Broken Boy

"Along the banks of Babylon's rivers, we sat as
exiles, mourning our captivity, and wept with
great love for Zion." (Psalm 137:1, TPT)

He didn't start out as the man I knew. My father, the rapist, child molester, abuser, and adulterer was once a little boy; a sweet innocent little baby boy. Many years ago, his family showed my mom and me a picture of him as a baby. He was sitting up in this picture with his curly hair atop his head. You could see his big brown eyes looking at the person taking his picture. I remember the picture so well. I remember his little diaper, the shirt he wore, and the baby slobber in the corner of the tiny lips of his slight grin. I remember thinking how I really couldn't imagine him that way, so needy and so precious, but he was. And in God's loving eyes, he still is. He wasn't always the man he became. He was broken along the way.

I am now a mother of three. Two of my children are boys. I have had a lot of time to think about the process of raising them. I am fully aware that everything said and done towards these young men has the power to help or harm them. I know what happens when too much hurt fills the space of your soul. I know how hard it can be to rise above the lies we are taught about ourselves. Even though it could seem that my dad is a completely different type of person than I am, I really understand him. In truth, his upbringing wasn't too different from mine. His parents both were church goers, and they were in ministry intermittently throughout their lives. His mother was very focused on Jesus. In fact, she too did community missions work in her later years. Rumors about abuse have circled through my dad's family, but there was a culture of secrecy. And growing up, while playing at the feet of chatty adults, I heard a lot about things that went on years before me.

When I heard them speak of sexual secrets and patterns of abuse from their youth, I didn't understand what any of that meant as a child. However, I never forgot it because it sounded awful enough to remember. I can also recall them discussing the sexual behavior of my dad and his brothers when they were young boys. Once again, I was very little and really wasn't sure what it all meant. I heard that my grandfather was awful to some of his kids and to my grandmother during their early years and when he left, not too many people were very sad about it. I imagine there were a lot of issues already in the family by the time my grandparents separated. However, by the time I was born, there must have been some level of reconciliation between my dad and his father. My grandfather had the opportunity to get to know my brothers and me before he died.

As I mentioned already, there was also sexual abuse in my dad's home when he was a child. When children are sexually exposed at a young age, they can role play it with other kids, even with family members. Oftentimes, it's done secretly because that's how they learned to do it, in secret. It was the secret and hush hush things the adults in those random conversations at my grandmother's house were talking about. There was no clarification on the details of those activities, which was probably for the best since I was listening. However, as an adult, it gives me clues into the background of the adult behavior of my father. You can't be sexually exposed as a child and walk away from it without a loss of innocence. Today, there are so many avenues for a child to become sexually exposed. Media, music, and pornography have increased the number of explicit landmines that people will encounter. Sexually explicit media can have the same mental and emotional effect on a person as someone else that experiences coerced and inappropriate human sexual encounters. Any level of inappropriate or forced sexual exposure requires a healing touch from God so that He can restore what was taken. It took me years to figure out what my family meant by the phrase "messed with." I believe that sometimes in families, the vocabulary that is used to address these serious issues hedges away from the full trauma of what it really is and what it does to a person. I don't lay any blame or negativity on my family in any way. Afterall, some of them were child victims of something that was much worse than the phrase "messed with" implies.

This may come as a surprise to some of you, but sexual play is actually very common amongst children who were coerced sexually or forced into sexual activity by another child or adult. In our world today, those things may also be accompanied by explicit sexual media. Once that coercing child or adult begins this with the victimized child, that victimized child is more likely to pass on the abuse to their siblings and friends. At first, it's not out of an intention to harm others, but because they now have a broken perspective of how to have fun, how to build relationships, how to deal with the sexual addiction that is developing inside of them, and how to show affection to those they care about.

I understand this very well. I had many children around me who had the same issues that I had. I know that they did because those children were often interested in sexual play. This brings up another important point. Abused children may also put out a vibe that draws other abused children and other abusers to them. I don't know why this is the case sometimes, but it is. When I was around seven or eight, we went to a friend's house for a large get together. There were lots of families there, and the adults wanted to talk and hang out. They sent all the children my age into the kids' room to watch *The Wizard of Oz*. When I went into the room, some of the boys were touching each other and engaging in group sexual activity. Without shame, they looked at me and invited me to join them. It was as if I wore a sign on my head that said, "use me." I can name several times in my life where I was taken to homes and gatherings and, without fail, I would be solicited for sex from another child. Sometimes, I would walk out and play alone, but sometimes the adults insisted I go play with the other children. That day at that gathering where the kids were supposed to be watching *The Wizard of Oz*, I was told that I had to stay with the kids. I didn't have any perception that I myself was abused, so it never occurred to me to report any specific activity to my mom about other kids. Even though I felt incredibly depressed often, I figured my depression was my own fault, and that I should get used to it. I believe this was part of my dad's journey as well.

Very few dirty secrets make their way to light in a family that pushes things under the rug that are difficult to process emotionally. Oh, maybe there is gossip here or there, but there is rarely a time when anyone says, "I am calling this sin out into the light." It's common for families that have had abuse to develop a family culture of keeping secrets. It's also very common for an abuser to only target one or a few children whom they feel they can control. That abuser will have a completely different, and seemingly healthy, relationship with other children in the same circle of family or friends. My dad did this. He only targeted me and my sister who lived with her birth mother most of her life. That was to his advantage since we had different moms and lived in different cities most of the time. My dad developed a "healthy man" persona in his relationships with most of the people at our church. This kind of scheming creates an environment for the victim to feel like they are the only one being abused, and that no one would believe them anyway. It also allows the abuser to have false testimony of who they really are. Those well-meaning people who have not been abused by the accused will often assume the victim, if they even try to speak up, is making things up. These people sometimes think an abused child is lying because their own experience with the abuser is so different.

The few times I tried to share what was going within my close social circle, I either was told I was making things up, told it wasn't a big deal, or I was told not to worry about it because my dad would stop eventually. Once, I told a group of people at my public high school, and one-by-one they all told me of all their abuse and rape experiences. There was no help there. I was telling all the wrong people for sure. I think that happens to abused children more than we'd like to realize. I have talked to other survivors of abuse since I've been older, and I have found that those of us who have been abused can sometimes see the signs of abuse in others a mile away. It stands out like a bullseye when I see certain behavior and mannerisms. My husband and I have offered support to families who foster and adopt children for many years, and I have noticed the signs of abuse in some of these children. You don't even have to read a report on them. They carry their wounds with them.

Abuse can continue when families protect the abusers by ignoring the obvious signs of the victims, and they choose to turn a blind eye to sketchy behavior. It's as if they plug their ears with their fingers, shut their eyes and say "la, la, la, nothing's going on there." These families do this, not out of a desire to cause more hurt, but out of a desire to avoid shame and embarrassment. I noticed these tendencies in my father's family growing up. Becoming honest and open about abuse of any kind is disruptive to the comfortable flow of life. No one wants those kinds of disruptions. Even as an adult, when I have shared with certain people in his family about what had happened to me, they have said things like, "He never treated me that way. He's been nice to me." And to be honest, I pulled away from those relationships. There are, of course, many in my dad's family who have believed me right away and without doubt. All my dad's brothers personally told me that they knew I was telling the truth. Two of them also apologized to me for what they knew my dad did to me. That means a lot to me even today. However, the family pride and the fear of exposure of dark deeds was too great for some of them to be willing to deal with at the time I was going through it. Unfortunately, that was the case, even for my dad's mom.

I remember being at her house after my dad beat me on the freeway, banging my head on concrete over and over. My dad had just finished preaching at a revival in Houston where he prayed over a woman that night who had demonic influences. She was delivered and left the meeting rejoicing. After the revival meeting, we then drove to my grandmother's house. It was on the way to her house that my baby brother had upset my dad. So what better way to handle the situation than to pull over in the fast lane to use me for a punching bag and bang my head on the concrete for a few minutes. My dad calmed down enough from his freeway rant to continue his drive. Over the freeway and through the woods to grandmother's house we went. Once there, I told my grandmother what happened. My father went into a shouting rage, expressing that he was not sorry. He told me I deserved everything that I got, right in front of my grandmother. He told me it was my fault that I was beaten, and it wouldn't have happened had I been different. He cooled down again, ultimately packed his bags, and left to spend a few days with my sister.

I was crying and my grandmother just told me that my father didn't mean it, and that I should just forgive him. My grandmother also said that it was going to be okay and that I should stop crying and try not to talk about it anymore. I loved my Grandmother and I know she loved me, so I believe that she probably felt helpless like my mom did. Or maybe that's how she learned to deal with those types of events in her own life experiences. I don't know, but it sure sent a message to me that I shouldn't let the truth of things out, that no one would help me, and that I would be blamed. There was always so much cover up in those days for all sorts of things in my life. I believe that many in my father's family have since moved into healing waters over the years. However, my father continued to hide behind the pulpit, work titles, and well-crafted lies most of his life. It made a mockery of the truth of who God really was to me. It was the revelation of Yeshua to me personally that allowed me to know who God was outside of what I was experiencing through my dad's spiritual leadership. Family pride can sometimes be a very destructive thing. It's an awful environment to grow up in when you are the victim of abuse. I believe my father experienced some of this abuse growing up.

I know it is an uncomfortable topic, but this is something that needs to be talked about. So many children have been abused sexually and don't have anyone to share all the feelings and emotions and desires that come from the abuse. Many feel ashamed to say that, even after some time of being abused, they begin to enjoy the feelings associated with the abuse. My father used to tell me, "If you didn't like it, you would've screamed. If you tell someone on me, they'd all know you enjoyed it." This is the trap that I believe Satan wants abused children to fall into: the trap of shame. The enemy of our soul doesn't want people to feel like they can talk honestly about what the abuse has done to their minds, souls, and identities. What if you just want to think and feel innocent again?

I know my dad struggled with this his whole life. I struggled with all those things for years myself. I know that my dad felt ashamed of these evil habits and addictions. I believe that he went through cycles of convincing himself he could control his destructive sexual thoughts, then give into it, only to feel angry afterwards. He hated who he had become and used the Bible and ministry to hide his own suffering soul issues. We saw it all the time in our home growing up. The pride and excitement he could feel when things were really moving well at church or at work, and the bouts of anger towards my mom or us kids, and the depression. He clearly struggled with depression. I wasn't aware of it fully as a child because I was often depressed myself. But when I think back on all my family memories with my dad, his emotions had extreme highs and long, deep, angry lows.

Most of all, he struggled with identity. I know from experience that it was his deepest struggle. How could you know who you are in God if you are trapped in a lie? He truly didn't understand who he was in God's eyes. He probably looked in the mirror many days and only saw a dirty old man who liked having sex with kids. God sees deeper than we see ourselves and God sees our calling and our potential. I know this because our childhoods really weren't that different, and I know what I struggled with. I saw myself as a child trapped in some twisted relationship with my dad. God saw the calling and potential of all that He had planned for me and wanted to pull that forth. And so, my heavenly Father came to me, and began to heal me and save me from the grave. I believe that God has been reaching out to my dad through the years, just like He was reaching out to me as a child.

My dad was a broken little boy. It didn't matter what his age was, how tall he became, if he was married or not to my God-fearing mom or to anyone else. Inside, he was still a broken boy. Damaged from the church hurt in his growing up, the abuse, the lies spoken into his life by the Enemy over the years. He struggled with acceptance and longed to be noticed as intelligent and wise. He would say phrases like, "you think you're smarter than me?" to my mom and to me as I got older. He would also often have me help him complete his college assignments and use my mother's skills and pass them off as his own. He loved titles, and was constantly seeking to oversee whatever he was involved in. He always felt threatened by my mom or me if we got too much praise from other people. If we did, he would treat us harshly, call us names like, "stupid," and tell my mom that she was an idiot and wouldn't make it without him. If I got accolades at school, he would downplay them and act like they didn't mean much. When I was graduating from high school, he said he might come to the graduation and sat there looking at the television in his house pants and old shirt. Sometimes he would tell me that no one would want to marry a person like me, or that I was stupid just like my momma. He constantly sought position, wanted honor, and was willing to push his family down to achieve it. He had a deep empty well that he longed to be filled with significance. It was so obvious from the outside, but he couldn't see it. He was trapped in a prison of his own making.

Only Jesus can set him free, not the little idol of Jesus that he made with his chisel of "my own way" and his clay of "this is what I think a loving god is." Only the real Jesus of the Bible, the one who loves and holds justice in his hands. The Jesus of the Word who is merciful and the one who will judge. I think my dad was afraid to step into a relationship with that Jesus. It required too much sacrifice on his part. He would have to become honest about who he is, what he's done, and who he's hurt along the way. He would have to lose the status and the public face he hides behind. He'd have to submit himself to others for help and accountability. I think for some people, the possible embarrassment is too great a cost than to live in truth, but they are wrong.

When you live in darkness everyone sees it. You aren't fooling anyone but yourself. You think you are, but one day you will face God. I would rather fight tooth and nail against the sins and addictions I've faced and meet my Lord saying I never gave up, rather than give in to sin and submit my life towards a direction of an eternal hell without grace, love, light, and freedom. However, when you are trapped in abusive behavior, you really are not thinking clearly enough to recognize the worth and freedom of Truth. My broken father never came into that reality during his time living with my mom, brothers and me. To this day, as far as I know, he still lives in his lies.

I forgave my father years ago. How could I not? All I must do is imagine he was one of my own sons. It's easy for me to feel deeply saddened for my dad living in the state he is in. He didn't start out the way he finished in our family. He started out an innocent child, just like I was. He took on shame, just like I did. He struggled with sexual tensions within, just like I did. He hated how he felt about sex and pleasure when he felt guilty, just like I did. He hated who he was and didn't know how to change, just like I did. He prayed for escapes at different seasons of his life and tried to get free on his own, just like I did. He hated his biological father for a long season, just like I did. He hid behind church and Christian activity, just like I did. However, that's where the similarities end.

I found my hope in the truth of God's word. I started my path of freedom when I stopped keeping secrets. I have allowed nourishing people into my world, counselors, and healthy ministers of the gospel of Christ, that have helped me to stay focused on my true identity in Yeshua and the reality of God's overwhelming love for me. I no longer carry shame, or a desire to be significant in man's eyes. I know that there is nothing I could do that would change the depth of God's love for me. I can't earn it, nor take it away. I know with certainty that Jesus is all the significance I need. He carries all the weight for me. I am His princess, and all my desires are met in Him. All I need to do is rest in him, trust Him with my hurt, my sins, and the dirty things of the past. And I have faith to trust God for the future that He has planned for me.

I keep a picture of myself as a baby laying naked and innocent on my baby blanket. I used to hate that picture. It used to make me feel sick inside. Now, I love it. I don't look at it and think of all the evil things that happened. Now when I see that picture, I am touched that God made me, and that He loves me, and that He has always seen me through the blood of Christ, just like that innocent baby in the picture. My prayer for my dad is that he gets real and honest about his life, seeks help outside of himself, and most of all, permits our good Father to wrap His big strong arms around that broken boy inside him, allowing the tender love of Jesus to heal him. If you need healing today, God wants to do the same for you. Crawl up on His big strong legs and let yourself be enveloped into his arms. Let the scent of His love saturate you and begin to heal you.

How to Escape a Fire

"Whoever has my commands and keeps
them is the one who loves me, and the
one who loves me will be loved by my
Father, and I will love him and reveal
myself to him." (John 14:21, CJB)

Life has a lot of warning moments. You know what I'm talking
about, those moments when you get that funny feeling or a thought
that maybe the choice you are about to make is not a good idea. Those
are warnings. Warnings of the potential fire that can, and probably
will, destroy some of the goodness in your life if you make certain
decisions. Most people recognize the general warnings of their lives.
It's the subtle ones we miss, the ones that Holy Spirit so gently gives
us, because God has better plans than we have for ourselves. I have
come to believe that learning to understand God's voice is the most
important navigating power I can have. Today, I don't even start my
day without asking the Lord to speak to me about how I should
go about my day. I draw myself into a womb with only Jesus so
that I can connect to His voice. After all, His sheep know His voice.
We can only know His voice if we spend time close to the Shepard.
Being familiar with the voice of God in our lives helps us to recognize warnings on seemingly insignificant choices that aren't generally
important to most people. These are the decisions that can make a
difference in how we escape a fire. Heeding these kinds of warnings
can impact the quality and quantity of our life.

I have experienced many warnings or promptings about things
in my life while growing up. Some I ignored and chalked up to just
a strange sensation or thought. Over the years I have come into the

reality that my Creator has been communicating with me my whole life. God has given me some unique warning moments to guide me in learning how to hear His voice in my life and circumstances. I found that God will use multiple ways to speak to me. It can be a dream, a vision, His voice, a verse he tells me to go to and read. No matter how God speaks to me, it's always in line with the Bible. He's even shown me symbols and written things down for me in dreams. But when he just speaks to me audibly or with an internal voice unlike mine, I know I need to pay attention.

The first time I really realized this was my freshman year of high school. I was standing at my locker getting my things ready to catch the bus and go home when I heard a voice tell me "get your math book." The voice even told me what pages to go over in the book. I had been hearing from God long enough at this point to know it was His word to me. However, I figured it wasn't all that important to do. Afterall, we had just started those sections of the book and I had plenty of time to work on it. I had no homework that night in math, so from the limited power of my tiny brain I said to God, "I will go over that tomorrow." I promptly closed my locker and went home. The next day my math teacher, who had had a busy night the day before, decided to give us all a quiz on the very pages that God told me to study. I laughed at myself. What a silly girl I was to believe that God's wisdom and promptings were only for the big issues and that I was better at judging what I thought were the insignificant ones. I learned a lesson I have never forgotten. When He speaks, do it.

This lesson has always stayed close to my heart, and it helped me to develop a better understanding of my position in my relationship with God. His sovereignty is not limited to the big moments of life, but it is more than enough for the everyday, seemingly mundane moments as well. I spent the next four years of my high school career becoming more aware of how Holy Spirit was leading me in the little things, as well as the big ones. This practice came in handy my sophomore year of college in Oregon. I was walking with an exchange student from Kenya. She and I were leaving the campus to go to a coffee house to hang out. We stood at the street corner where the stop light was and waited for the walk sign to light up. This was a very busy street. It was the main street through town, so big trucks and cars alike used it to travel to the nearby cities. We were lost in our conversation when suddenly I heard a voice tell me to fall to the ground with my friend now! This voice was loud and urgent inside of me, and I knew it was God. Without hesitation I pushed her to the ground. She was startled but as we lay there, I heard the loud noise of the cars and I looked back at my feet. I saw the wheels of a diesel truck that had suddenly lost control less than an inch from our toes as it plowed through the street sign and stoplight. It left its wheel tracks where we had been standing. My friend and I instantly began to praise God. I now use this experience with young people often as an example of the importance of learning how God speaks to us and obeying what He says. When we obey God, we not only have a better life, but in general, we live longer. We are able to navigate the fires that can potentially burn us out of the plans God has for us.

Sometimes fires come regardless of our obedience, but we don't have to be overtaken by them. In between college during the summer months, I would come home and stay with my mom and brothers, who at this point were now free from the abuse of my dad. My parents had divorced at this point. These were the glory days of my youth. Yes, they were hard for my mom sometimes, but I am certain she didn't mind. All the difficulties we would face as a family after my dad was gone were well worth the journey. He chose not to be a healthy member of our family. Therefore, we moved forward in peace. When I came home in the summers between college, my mom, brothers, and I did as much as we could to be joyful. We had park trips with neighboring children, potlucks with church friends, and video game parties with some of the kids from youth group. We had slumber parties and stayed up all night during sleep overs. We didn't have to sneak around anymore. It was wonderful, but I also had to work.

My mom and I were the only income in our household, so we worked together to make ends meet. My mom was the main income for my family, but I helped however I could during the summers. I typically found work through a temp agency. I had found it was a great way to get a decent paying summer job with my current credentials at that time. On a particular morning during one of these summers, I had great hesitations about driving the car that my mom had purchased for me. This was because the night before I had a dream, and I knew it was from God. In the dream, I was driving my car to or from work down the freeway and it made a funny noise and caught on fire. The whole thing just burned. All my senses were turned on in this dream, so I felt the heat. I wasn't in the car while it was burning. In the dream, I was suddenly taken outside of the car and was standing looking at it burn. It was scary. Thus, when I awoke, I had no intention of driving it. I told my mom I was concerned about driving the car and asked if I could drive her minivan to work instead. She said I could. I figured from all my previous experience in understanding God's voice in my life, I didn't want to assume it was a 'pizza' dream and end up in a burning car. Part of me didn't think it would really happen, but in keeping with practicing obedience I had enough concern of the possible reality to just obey the fire warning. I had just purchased and paid for the installation of a CD player and new stereos with a 6 CD changer in that car.

My mom drove the car that day instead. I got a call from her while I was at work telling me that she and my brothers decided to go somewhere and used my car, since that was the only one left to use. She called me as my car engine was on fire. She pulled over on the highway and the firemen came. They made sure everyone was safe, and I think my brother even got to sit on the firetruck. While on the phone with my mom, I reminded her about my new CD player, so we prayed that it would be spared the damage that was happening from the fire. It may sound like a silly prayer to some, but one thing I've learned through the years is that there is no prayer too small or weird for God. I am happy to say that the CD player with 6 CD changer came out of it alive and unburnt. Several years later, when my youngest brother was old enough to get a car, I gave that CD player to him, and he got it installed in his car. It's possible that no one in my family could have escaped that fire unscathed had we not heard, understood, and followed the voice of God that day to move us into His plan of safety. This is our reality as believers in Jesus; God has goodness and mercy for us in big things like a car fire, and even in little things like a car CD player. If you aren't sure how to recognize the voice of the Shepard in your life, then I encourage you to dig into the Word. Yeshua is the Living Word, so know what the Word says about Him and what it says about you. Fall in love with Him and go deep with Him and you will get to know His character. Ask Holy Spirit to fill you with a passion for the love letter we have from God, the Bible. If we can embrace the overwhelming love and wonderful thoughts that He has for us, we can draw deeper into His love and hear Him more clearly in our lives.

Fathered

"Out of my deep anguish and pain I prayed,
and God, you helped me as a father. You came
to my rescue and broke open the way into a
beautiful and broad place." (Psalm 118:5, TPT)

Growing up with a dysfunctional dad can leave a person feeling fatherless. I tried to find a way to have healthy associations with him and tried to build a relationship with him that wasn't excessively destructive, but it proved impossible. I ended up hurt and abused in my efforts, and found myself wishing I had a different dad all together or that he was dead. But God is a refuge for the fatherless. This statement could seem like meaningless words when you feel like you are alone in your pain. However, the reality of that truth can come through people that are led by Holy Spirit to bring light and hope into our dark circumstances. I had a deep, empty hole where a dad was meant to be. God met my need. Throughout my life, God has fathered me using exceptional men who had a heart for the orphaned soul.

The earliest of these men was Mr. Hills. I would have had very negative perspectives of all men early on had it not been for him. He was one of my teachers for nine plus years at my Christian school in Texas. He was a tough, former football player, well over six feet tall, built for sports, and didn't take garbage from anyone. He grew up in Michigan and knew how to ice skate very well. He clearly had a northern culture that was vastly different than the southern culture I was so familiar with. He and his wife were always there for me. I loved my time with Mr. Hills. I would often imagine that he was my real dad when I was with him. I understood that he wasn't. However, it made me feel good just pretending. I learned how to feel safe with a man being with him all those years. God's placement of him in my life was vital for my future healing and my development as a young girl. I am so blessed to have been Fathered by Mr. Hills. He's older now, but still going strong. I love him very much.

Sometimes, the most unlikely people will be used by Holy Spirit to move in fatherhood towards a child. After my family moved from Texas to Washington, I started attending public schools. We moved around a lot during that time. However, there was one school where I spent most of my high school years. It was there that God brought Mr. Wilson into my life. Mr. Wilson was a math teacher. He seemed to have a sense that I was in trouble at home. Mr. Wilson would often let me hang out with him in class as we talked about math. He would help me with my work and was always so kind to me when I was having a difficult day. I felt so close to him. I eventually found out that he was a believer in Jesus and was very active in serving Christ. I began to talk to him about some of the non-abusive stress in my home. Mr. Wilson sometimes would pray with me if I asked him to. I felt so safe in his classes. Many of the kids who attended his class were so disruptive, but even then, I knew that I was in a very safe place when I was with him. Furthermore, he was very forgiving and kind, even to the difficult students. I loved talking to Mr. Wilson. He was full of care and compassion to all his students. I don't even think he had kids, but he sure knew a lot about fatherhood. I pray for Mr. Wilson whenever I think of him.

After high school, I went to a small Quaker college in Oregon. George Fox College (now University) proved to be a perfect fit for me. There were so many men who spoke life to me during my college years, but I want to highlight two of them, Pastor Gregg Lamm and Dr. Dale Orkney. When I first arrived, Pastor Lamm truly fathered me in a time when I was not only fatherless, but I was starting a journey of filing charges of sexual and physical abuse against my father. This, to say the least, was a time when my heart was so open and raw. I needed a man in my life to hug me and tell me I was going to make it through. He was that man. He helped me with so many things during that season, even practical things. He took me to town and showed me how to set up a bank account. I had never flown on a plane before, and he paid for a ticket for me to get to my court date. He invited me to his home just to hang out with his family. I needed all of that. Pastor Gregg Lamm helped usher me into my season of freedom.

As my college years went by, I developed a beautiful relationship with Dr. Dale Orkney. I loved that man. He always dressed like he was in the 1950's. He had a buzz cut, and he always wore a smile. I probably spent more time with him than any other professor at George Fox. I loved to just hang out in his office and chat with him. He was a family man. He kept pictures of his family all around his office. He also loved to travel, and he loved plants. He was a Botanist. I was a science major and took several of his classes. He was an outdoorsman, and I loved that too. He loved Jesus. Oh, how he loved Jesus. And he loved his wife. He loved to talk about her often. It seems insignificant, but all these things deeply ministered to me. I was fathered in ways that were deeper than I understood at the time I was in college, but that would carry me throughout my life shaping my reality of what a man and husband looked like.

After my college years, I worked for a while and ultimately ran into Paul from high school again in Sears. We hung out for three weeks to catch up on old times, then he asked me to marry him. We got married in 2000 on the most beautiful day of that year in a rose garden, the same one we went to on our first date. Paul's wonderfulness is, in part, because he has an amazing father. My husband's father is currently the powerful father influence I have in my life now. I watched how he loved my mother-in-law. I took mental notes on how he so deeply sacrifices for his children and grandchildren. I never saw that growing up from my father. To be so close to this kind of love is an amazing thing for me. Furthermore, to be married to Paul, who shares so many of the characteristics of his dad, is a great miracle in my life. I have seen the legacy that Paul has through his father and his grandfather. I live every day the fulfilment of the fruit of all their sacrifices and steadfast commitment to Jesus our Lord. I am honored that I get to raise sons that will continue in this blessing and carry on the ministry of fatherhood to children they will influence and shape. I have learned the most about how to leave a legacy that counts from my father-in-law. I love him more than he will ever know. Who would my Paul have been without him?

I have been tremendously blessed to have all these amazing men speak God's goodness in my life. Life is so valuable, and love is so healing. Even if it is just a kind word or act of compassion, everything we do for Christ matters. I pray that more men, whether they have been a father or not, would step into opportunities to be the hands and feet of Jesus to a young girl or boy in their circle of influence. You may think your actions are insignificant, but they are not. You could end up being one of the few, or only, positive male role models that a child will have.

It's always amazing how God works all things for good for those who love Him. You may not ever find out this side of heaven the impact you had, but continue the good race in love and practice fatherhood when Holy Spirit leads you. I promise you this, you will have a few surprises waiting for you in heaven.

"But who am I, and who are my people, that we should be able to give as generously as this? For everything comes from You, and we have given You only what comes from Your own hand." (1 Chronicles 29:14, HCSB)

"For God is not unjust; He will not forget your work and the love you showed for His name when you served the saints— and you continue to serve them." (Hebrews 6:10, HCSB)

"But you, God, see the trouble of the afflicted. You consider their grief and take it in hand. The victims commit themselves to you; you are the helper of the fatherless." (Psalms 10:14, NIV)

Becoming

Gratitude

"Don't worry about anything, but in everything,
through prayer and petition with thanksgiving,
let your requests be made known to God.
And the peace of God, which surpasses every
thought, will guard your hearts and minds
in Christ Jesus. Finally brothers, whatever is
true, whatever is honorable, whatever is just,
whatever is pure, whatever is lovely, whatever
is commendable—if there is any moral
excellence and if there is any praise—dwell
on these things." (Philippians 4:6-8, HCSB)

I am grateful for many people and opportunities in my life. I want to live my life in a way that honors God's Word and the investment of love I have received from so many. Many times my emotions want to wander into waters of discontentment, which leads me to a lack of gratitude for who and what I have in my life. But Holy Spirit always brings me into truth. It has taken some effort over the years to take a grateful seat in difficult circumstance and situations that aren't going the way I planned. However, I find that by refocusing my thoughts and turning my heart to good things that come from God I can overcome my instinct to worry, blame, and complain. Holy Spirit is helping me every day to walk this out.

On my birthday, years ago before we had children, I had made all these plans for what I wanted to do that day. My mom had always made a huge deal out if it, so I had pretty high expectations. Unfortunately, my husband Paul had to work and so I was going to have to delay my plans. A faithful friend that I had during that season of my life stopped by that morning and said that she wanted to take me out for my birthday. Now you would assume that I would have been happy that my friend remembered my birthday and took the time to surprise me like that. I wasn't. In my heart I was so bummed out about my original plans changing that I found myself complaining in my head about the new plans. Nevertheless, as Paul went to work, I got my coat and purse and headed out with my friend. She took me all over the downtown area, shopping, eating, and taking in the sites. It was one big shopping spree. I had never gone to most of the stores before and saw many places in my little town that I had never noticed. I should have been having a blast. Instead, I was pouting about my broken dreams for the day. It was during our lunch break at a café that it just hit me like a ton of bricks. I had been so incredibly ungrateful all day long! God had brought someone to come and bless me on my birthday, and I had spent the first few hours of it sulking. Right away I asked the Lord to forgive me for my lack of gratitude. I then let my friend know just how grateful I really was. We had a wonderful rest of the day. That is one of my most memorable birthdays.

Even when horrible things happen, finding our way to a place of gratefulness can help change the tide of how we experience our circumstances. Once our moving truck, containing everything we owned, and our car being towed behind it was stolen. It ranks in my book as one of my most interesting traumatic experiences. We were in shock for the first day or so. Eventually, all the emotions began to pile in. I found it a real challenge to keep my thoughts focused on the good things that God was doing at first. But the more I thought of His faithfulness, and recognized His love through others, the pain of the loss we had experienced didn't hurt so bad. I find that focusing myself on the good produces a path for joy to flow, even when things are stressful. Some situations can't change very easily. However, it's more important to focus on how we respond than focusing on how bad we feel. If you follow your sad and bad feelings, you will drown in your tears, pulling others down to drown with you. Grab a lifeline from Holy Spirit, swim back to shore, and focus on the truth of God and His word. What I've found is that your feelings catch up to reality eventually. That alone can be make the difference of whether we experience peace or devastation in hard circumstances.

When I was very young, my mom threw a big birthday party for me. To be honest, she always gave me big birthday parties, but this one stands out due to my lack of gratitude. My mom had invited my cousins, my neighbors, and everyone at my church. I had a hula hoop and had been practicing with it over the last few weeks prior to this party. I thought I had gotten pretty good at it. Everyone at the party was having a great time playing and I wanted them all to stop what they were doing to watch me. I couldn't get a big enough group together at one time to watch me. My thoughts started down a complaining, sulky road. Ultimately, I found myself sitting in the house somewhere with a frown on my face and tears in my eyes. I was literally missing my own birthday party because everyone wasn't doing what I wanted them to do.

When my mom noticed me having my little fit, she graciously made an announcement to everyone in the garage playing that it was time for them to watch me use my hula hoop. Everyone stopped what they were doing and stared. All eyes were on me. My mom hunched over me and said, "Go on, do it." Suddenly, I realized how un-fun this really was. I did show them my skills, but in showing them I realized that I really wasn't that good. Furthermore, I had missed a fair chunk of my own birthday celebration complaining about people not watching me. I was more bummed from feeling so embarrassed after they all watched me. I spent a few minutes refocusing my thoughts to the reality that everyone there was to celebrate me and my life and that I didn't have to waste my emotions on sadness or embarrassment. Eventually, I did get myself together and enjoyed the rest of my birthday party. In the end, I realized how grateful I was to all my friends and family who came that day. I was shown a lot of love, despite my moments of stinky attitude. Isn't that how Jesus is with us? He keeps on loving us regardless. He gives us mercy in our mess.

If you've ever watched the "Filling Station," a show written by Ms. Jane E. Dickerson highlighting Biblical principles for kids, then you've seen Howard Auto-Bee. It's a little skit where there is a

Bee/man in cartoon form who visits cartoon kids who are struggling with various issues. He always would teach them a quick lesson and then everyone would sing "mmm, learn to be humble bees." Well, I was watching "The Filling Station" late one night when the Howard Auto-Bee segment of the show came on. In that segment, a girl was sitting under a tree complaining and grumbling about herself and others. Howard Auto-Bee buzzed over and suggested that instead of counting all the negative things, she should count all the awesome things in life. He suggested that she make a list identifying all the blessings around her. The girl began to make her list and as she did, her emotions began to shift. Even though I was watching this with my children, it pierced right through my soul. I realized that I wasn't always a humble bee. I had many occasions where I had allowed my mind to go down long trails of complaining. In fact, I noticed over the next few weeks after that show, how I naturally fall into those common negative ways of thinking. You must fight those damaging thoughts with Truth, which is the Word of God, and gratitude.

Here is part of my grateful list:

1. Jesus. Oh, how He loves me so. My defender, my peace, my greatest love.
2. Paul, my husband. His faithfulness, lavish love towards me, and passion for Christ has been healing to me.
3. Mom. Her love for Jesus is contagious. She leaves beauty wherever she goes. She taught me how to be woman of God.
4. Lynette. I learned so much as she grew into a young lady. Her passion and zeal for God continues to motivate me daily.
5. My sons. They keep me young and in touch with the world around me. I love the blessings of each day I have with them. They keep laughter alive in our home.
6. My granddaughter. She is the mango of my eye! I see the beauty of her momma in her.

Having an attitude of gratitude allows us to see the best in others and our circumstances. It brings us closer to peace and closer to Yeshua since He is our Sar Shalom, The Prince of Peace. All of us struggle from time to time with complaining and ungratefulness. Some people have a habit of grumbling about everything and have difficulty recognizing the blessings they've been given. If you fit any of these categories, you are not stuck. When we renew our minds with the word of God and walk humbly like Howard Auto-Bee suggests, we will find our way to a path of gratitude. And when that happens, we will be healthier in any situation we face. Shalom.

Becoming a Family

"'For my thoughts are not your thoughts,
neither are your ways my ways,' declares
the LORD." (Isaiah 55:8, NIV)

"Trust in the Lord with all your heart and
lean not on your own understanding; in all
your ways submit to him, and he will make
your paths straight." (Proverbs 3:5-6, NIV)

Becoming parents was a journey for my husband Paul and me. Our second year of marriage, we decided to go on a Kenyan adventure. Paul would teach math at Daystar University, and I would visit some orphanages and the hospitals. One place that really had an impact on both of us was Mother Teresa's in Huruma, Kenya. There was row after row of little beds where the babies slept. We spent some time holding the babies and decided that we wanted to adopt from there later.

When we returned to the United States, we began praying about our future adoption. Around this same time, I had a dream that Paul and I lived somewhere where there were trees, a cabin type house that had a porch, and a man with dark, curly and wavy hair wearing a business suit stood on the porch. In the dream I knew his name. It was Josiah. Josiah saw me walking up to the house and yelled, "Mom!" I knew that this man was my son and my heart leapt with joy! Then I woke up.

By the time we had been married almost five years, we started making plans to go back to Kenya and adopt from Mother Teresa's. We never really tried to get pregnant. I think I was afraid of bringing a child into this world. We got the picture of our soon-to-be adopted child from the Sisters of Charity. They had chosen a precious little boy for us that was two years old. He looked nothing like the man in my dream, but I knew this little boy was chosen by God for us to love. Paul and I knew we would give him another name, since it was currently Franciose. The Sisters of Charity were from all over the world and came up with the most creative names for the babies in their care.

It was an exciting time for us and a lot of work to prepare for all the different details involved in the process. In 2006, we moved to Kenya to complete our adoption process. We only planned to live there as long as it took to complete the adoption of our son, who had just turned three. If you have never adopted, then you may not believe me, but this is true. I know it's true because I have also given birth, so I say this with confidence. You know that feeling you get when you find out you are pregnant for the first time? That reality that births you into parenthood? And that awe you experience when you first see your baby on ultrasound or feel the baby move... I experienced all of those the moment we arrived at the airport and saw our son for the first time as we were exiting the gate. I was born that moment. I became a mom. That's a moment no one can take from me. I hadn't been pregnant before that time of my life, but after I did experience pregnancy and birth, I realized that the feelings were the same for me.

Our son, Michael (formerly Franciose), was named after Paul. Paul's full name is Michael Paul Holmes. He was from the slums of Huruma. His birth mother, probably a girl with many life troubles, threw him out of a moving car in the slum while his umbilical cord was still attached. He was born very premature. So much so, his fingernails had not yet developed. The Sisters of Charity took him to the orphanage, prayed for him, and nursed him to health and wellness. They chose him for us. We were honored to be his mommy and daddy. We were able to take him with us right away and as we grew as a family, we also grew in our faith. We needed heavenly help. There was so much more going on than we realized.

While we were living in Kenya, we worked at a home for street children. On the day we arrived at the home, we met our future daughter, but didn't know it yet. She had run away from the home with another girl. The other girl had her plans, but our daughter had a prayer in her heart. She said that she had a dream within her that God would give her parents from America and that she felt that if she walked in the direction of the bus station God would bring her parents there. Little did she realize, that's exactly where we would meet. We just didn't know what God had in mind at that moment. She, like many Kenyan children with little education, did not understand how far off America was. Many people in that area had little education and believed that America was somehow just over the mountains. I can remember telling the street kids who came to the home that the earth was round. Many didn't believe me. We ended up taking our daughter to the only library where we were in that part of Kenya, which happen to be run by a Catholic school, to show her a globe and the real distance between Kenya and America.

Once we were settled into the home for street kids, our future daughter got stung by a bee in the eye and she was in a lot of pain. We had brought some medications from the United States with us and Paul used them to help her heal. He also took her a banana to eat. I had a dream around that time, and in the dream I was shown my daughter's bee stung face. The voice of an angel said to me, "This is your daughter." I woke up. The next day, Paul wanted to have a serious talk with me. He said to me that he believes God is calling us to adopt not just our son, but one of the girls at the home. I asked if he had one in mind. He said, "Yes! Linet." I told him that I didn't know who Linet was, but that God did tell me in a dream that I was the mom of the girl with the bee stung eye. Paul got excited and said, "That's Linet!" We then called our adoption agency in the United States after talking to the family that ran the home for these street kids. We began the process of adopting not just one child, but two. There was excitement and joy for us during these days. After some legal paperwork was established, we then had two children in our home in Kenya. These were the days of mystery for me. I knew in my spirit that every moment mattered. Holy Spirit kept telling me that every moment mattered and to embrace the present.

We had so many adventures as a family. This really was a blessed time. I learned so much about raising a pre-teen girl. We changed our daughter's name from Linet to Lynette when she was around ten years old. We had to make up her birthday. She and Paul picked the date together. Our son and daughter learned how to be siblings. Our daughter learned how to be a daughter, which is not an easy journey when you've been living on the streets for many years. At the same time, we were learning how to parent.

We always knew we would homeschool our children. That included our kids in Kenya. Both Paul and I attended public and private schools growing up. We even had a chance to teach at both types of schools. Thus, we were aware of all those various school settings. My mom homeschooled me during my earliest years, and that really stuck with me as the most valuable learning time I had next to my Christian school years.

We loved the time of becoming a family and growing together with Michael and Lynette. We took them on wonderful outings and read together and played together. When the other street kids would come from school, our kids would play with them and we'd all watch movies on the VCR that was there. Paul would sometimes buy ice cream. The kids in the home loved that. Once Paul made homemade doughnuts and french fries for the kids. We always tried to come up with fun things to do with them. Sometimes, we would include the other kids in our homeschool science projects. We made a giant black solar balloon out of garbage bags and sent a message into the wilds of East Africa. This really freaked out the locals, seeing a giant black balloon float over their heads. We would have great conversations with the kids, such as explaining to them that Star Wars was not real, and that there wasn't an epic battle going on in space. I cherish those days.

There was so much going on in this season of our life. I was on a grand journey of falling in love with a little boy named Michael who fought hard at first against my love. I didn't give up. Lynette attached to me without many problems at all. We were soon a mom/daughter duo and loved being together. With Michael, it was much more complex. He refused to call me anything at first. In the beginning, he wanted me, but then he began to make it clear that he wasn't sure if he wanted me to be his mom. I knew it probably had something to do with growing up with lots of nuns who mothered him and very few father figures. Michael instantly embraced his baba's (daddy's) love. Michael loved having a dad so much I think he didn't want me in the middle of that at first. Therefore, Paul and I made a point to do things together with Michael all the time. It allowed him to learn what it meant to have a mom and dad and to be in a family. We even all slept in the same bed. Imagine, two adults sleeping on the edges of a bed and two children crammed in the middle. That was our family! Paul was Michael's heart. Michael wanted to be with his daddy all the time. So did Lynette. She and Michael used to fight over who was going to sit or sleep next to their dad. It usually ended in tears and Paul would have to find creative ways to make them both feel like he was near. I was on a journey of winning Michael's heart. It did happen, but at a time when I least expected it.

As I mentioned, having a dad was a big deal for our kids. Once, when Paul needed to make plans to get some legal documents from the tribal chief of my daughter's tribe, the kids overheard him talking about possible plans to leave for a day or two to see the chief. Both Lynette and Michael started crying and wailing. I asked them what was wrong, and they said that Baba was leaving for a few days. I explained to them that he would be back and that I was there. Lynette replied with a cry, "But who will take care of us? Baba does every-thing for us!" Slightly annoyed, I said, "I will!" They didn't seem to believe me. So, Paul sent someone in his place and he stayed. I smile now when I think of that whole scenario. Thinking back on it, Paul really did do most things for us. He filtered the rainwater and well water each day, which we used for drinking, bathing, and laundry. He walked to the market each day and cooked breakfast and lunch each day. He played with the children and read to them each day. He orchestrated all the big outdoor adventures we had. I did a lot also, but not the heavy lifting things. Part of the reason why I was so limited in the help I provided was because I was sick. I wasn't well for a few reasons, one being that I was pregnant and didn't know it. In fact, I didn't find out until I was almost six months along.

The sicker I got, the more concerned my family became for me. Michael would even bring me bananas in the mornings sometimes when I couldn't get out of bed. Eventually, Paul thought I should get a pregnancy test just to rule out all the possibilities. We had to go all over town before we were able to find a pregnancy strip for testing. It was positive. We were shocked. There was no place in our town to find prenatal vitamins. Also, there was no place to get an ultrasound. I was in pain all the time. I was also losing weight. I lost 74 pounds during this time. Paul and Lynette were worried. Through it all, we kept doing our best to love our children well. We took them to church and community events through the week. We taught them how to prepare new foods. They ate apples, pancakes, and chili for the first time with us. We poured ourselves out for them as best as we could even though finances were very low, and my body was sick. We were a happy, busy family, and worked through our daily trials in faith. One day, since there were worms in our water, we decided we should take a de-wormer. Paul read the label on the package and it said it was an "embryo-toxic," meaning it will kill an unborn baby. We were so glad we had taken that pregnancy test already. Otherwise, we wouldn't have known that I couldn't take the de-wormer. God had His hands on all our plans. I was so grateful He did. It was around this same time that we also began to run into problems in the adoption process of our two children. This glorious season quickly became one of the most traumatic times of our adult life together. It became a time to step into the heart of God's love, trusting that His ways were truly higher than ours.

God gave me several dreams during this season. One stands out well. In this dream, Paul and I were living in an apartment with a baby. I began to call out for my daughter and son Michael. My daughter called me in the dream on the telephone. She wasn't in our apartment with us. In fact, she was in the same apartment building but in a different apartment and for some reason I couldn't get to her. I was upset by this and asked her where Michael was because we couldn't find him in the apartment, nor had we heard of him being in any other apartment. In the dream. my daughter told me that Michael was gone. I screamed and began to cry uncontrollably in the dream. I woke up crying and in much pain. I told my family the dream. Lynette said to me after I told the dream, "Momma, maybe God is telling you that Michael will leave us."

I really didn't want to accept that. In fact, I told her that I refuse to accept that idea and that I was going to pray. Lynette was very wise for a child. She had already experienced the death of her own mother and had experienced very severe physical abuse and traumas of all kinds by the time we became her parents. She also had some experience hearing from God, and I think she had crossed the impossible bridges of life several times already and knew that no one was exempt from pain. My struggle was that I just didn't know how I would go on if I lost my children. This seemed to me, like the most unheavenly plan possible for my life. And yet, it's exactly what God had planned. The invitation of that dream, as well as many, was to trust God's path. "Do you trust me?" I was left with that question each time I had a dream during this time. Yet, I found myself wondering, "How do I trust a plan that is so devastating?" The answer is, one faith step at a time. I had to come to terms with the fact that when I surrendered my life to Christ, I was giving Him everything. Even my dreams, hopes, goals, and all that was precious to me. I was reminded in the Word that Jesus is my greatest prize and treasure, not my husband, children, or goals. I began to embrace the reality that God loved my family much more than I ever could, and that His love was perfect, even if my human perspective could only fathom what seemed right in my own eyes. I had to make a decision within my heart to believe that God's ways are better always. I would embrace every moment and thank Him for choosing me for the journey. I began to get into the scriptures that reminded me of this. I realized that I was but His servant and would go wherever Holy Spirit decided to guide my life. I would rather die in God's plans than live in my own. This was to be a faith crossing that would change me forever.

On our last court date, all our adoption planning fell through. Our lawyer, who was nonresponsive via email or phone, refused to return my calls. Everything had been shut down in the courts. All international adoptions to the U.S. had been stopped. They now had some newly formed, bizarre "adoption committee" that had to select who would be adopted to the U.S. Our kids were now unadoptable by us. On that day, I was numb. We all were. What do you do next? How do you keep being a family? We felt so lost, so hurt, so angry. Also, I was in so much physical pain all the time. We prayed and just kept on living as best as we could. We knew eventually, the money would run dry. At that point, we and our extended families had sold many things to allow us to keep living in Kenya. Generous friends had donated money and paid for food, rent, and even some of our adoption fees up to that point. We knew we couldn't continue to stay, but how could we leave our children? Where would they go? Everything seemed broken, and we didn't know how to fix any of it. We trusted God and knew He loved us, but we were so wounded inside and didn't know how to take a next step. God used Paul's mom's best friend, Linda Reno, to give a message to us through Paul's mom. Linda is one of those women who hears from God very clearly. When she gets a Word from the Lord, you want to hear what it is. Paul's mom called us and shared the word with us. Basically, God showed her that we needed to leave Kenya right away and to trust Him to care for our children. This word was confirmation to all the dreams I had gotten and what Paul knew in his heart. Upon getting that word, we did what we thought we couldn't do. We made a plan to leave our children in Kenya and go back to the United States.

How do you leave your children? You don't. You take them with you in your heart with tears and a belief that God's love is more powerful than yours. We found a missionary family to house our daughter Lynette temporarily until we got something more permanent. This began many years of paying people and boarding schools to take care of her for us. To this day, we literally communicate with her everyday over the cell phone. Our son Michael wasn't from the streets. He was from an orphanage. Therefore, we had to take him back to the orphanage. I am writing all of this rather calmly in words. But let me inform you, up until last year, I couldn't even bring any of this up without crying through the whole thing. I leave it to your heart to interpret all the emotions that we felt during this week of transition for us. My words can't do it justice to convey the level of emotional pain and grief we all went through. We went to Nairobi near the airport and stayed at the Seventh-Day Adventist guest house. Paul took both the kids with him when he took Lynette to the missionary family back at the missionary center. That was my last time hugging her before she left. I was too sick to go. It was upon the return of Paul and Michael to Nairobi that Michael really let go of all reservations of fighting his love for me. He saw me down the hall and ran to me yelling "mama!" That night, for the first time, he wanted me to sleep closest to him. He had really missed me. The saddest part of all was that the next day we had to take him back to the orphanage. Imagine the horror in my heart. I cried all night after Michael fell asleep. The next day, we called a taxi to take us back to Huruma, the slum where the orphanage is. The whole way there, Michael wanted to hold my hand. When we arrived at the orphanage there were other nuns from out of the country there that saw us and saw our son Michael. Though we were crying and clearly upset, they just rejoiced and smiled saying how wonderful it was to see how God creates families. One sister said she thought it was so beautiful, us being who we were together, loving and crying together. She saw God's story in us. It's taken me some years to see it, but now I can see and appreciate how beautiful it was and continues to be in our lives.

After leaving the orphanage, we had about three hours to wait before our plane flew out towards London. I was in so much pain on all levels, and was having massive contractions, even though I was only about 25 weeks pregnant. Paul and I sat at a little café and waited out the time in tears sitting in the corner of a balcony. People were staring at us while we sat and cried. We prayed and just wept when, suddenly, a little bird came and sat right on Paul's shoulder. We both felt the presence of God and knew He was speaking to us that He was Emmanuel. He was with us, He was carrying us, He was pouring His love out on us, even in our tears. Ultimately, we went to the airport, and stood in line to get on the plane. I was 6 months pregnant, in preterm labor about to give birth. I didn't know I was in labor of course, because I was always in pain. I was grieving and emotionally shot. But as I approached the doorway to our plane, I stood there with both hands on the doorway. I closed my eyes and I told God, "This is my worship to you, God. My full surrender. As I step on this plane, I will worship you." All our plans that year spiraled into a direction we didn't know how to come back from. But God was with us. He continues to be with us. Nothing was done that He didn't know about. My whole life, God has spoken so clearly to me. He chose to allow us this journey with very little insight about the outcome. He birthed us into parenthood in a Kenyan Airport. He trusted us with loving two children who are no longer orphans now. He grew our hearts in ways that only this journey could have done. We didn't need to know all the details. We just needed to trust Him. That's faith. God always has bigger plans that extend beyond our perception and space. I am grateful that we trusted Him. Even when it hurts. I know more about worship now from that season of my life than any other.

Waiting in the Miracle

"Indeed, Yahweh will comfort Zion, restore
her, and comfort all her broken places. He will
transform her wilderness into the garden of
Bliss, her desert into the garden of Yahweh. Joy
and laughter will fill the air with thanksgiving
and joyous melodies." (Isaiah 51:3, TPT)

We were on an emotional ride in 2006–2007. My husband Paul
and I had been transformed into the parents of two amazing children
in Africa that ended with us taking our son back to an orphanage
because of the change of laws there, and leaving our daughter with a
missionary family temporarily. In addition, I had become pregnant
while in Africa and was having a very high-risk pregnancy, though I
didn't find out until I returned to America. Most people start labor
and end labor within the city they live in. I started pre-term labor
in East Africa. I got on a plane and flew over to London, going to
the bathroom often on the plane ride to go number two, but all the
while almost pushing that premature baby out without knowing it.
I then had a ten-hour layover in London, in labor. I didn't know I
was in labor. I was just so miserable and couldn't understand why, no
matter how hard I pushed, going to the bathroom eluded me so. I
was in so much pain. Lastly, we took our final flight to Seattle where
our parents lived. My mother decided I should see a doctor as soon
as possible. I remember my sister-in-law crying when she first saw
me because she said I had lost so much weight and didn't look six
months pregnant. A day and a half later, after landing on U.S. soil, I
found myself in a doctor's office having an ultrasound.

No nurse believed me before this ultrasound that I was 6 months pregnant because I had lost around 74 pounds in Kenya. The first nurse that saw me was working with a Planned Parenthood office through the medical building I went to for medical help. This nurse was a tall, middle-aged blond who wore the traditional scrubs and gave intermittent smiles during her short questions to me. When I shared my story of just coming from Africa and being six months pregnant, she told me she didn't believe me and said to me, "Well we will see." I felt like she basically was calling me a liar. She had to give me my pregnancy test before I could continue in my medical help. After it came out positive, she told me that she still didn't believe I was six months and that I should have an abortion. I laughed in my head. I didn't expect that response from a nurse, but she's not the first person I had ever met that wanted to destroy part of me, so she didn't intimidate me.

I told her no. She told me to think about it in an authoritative tone, to which I again laughed to myself and told her that I wasn't going to kill my baby. She looked at me annoyed and gave me the papers I needed to get the medical help I was seeking. I wondered how many women followed the plans of that nurse for their children's lives. I pray for every family she helped to dismantle. I pray for this nurse that Holy Spirit will open her heart to truth and heal whatever wounds have led her to this. The next lady that helped me at this health office was a brown-haired twenty-something, who was no taller than five feet. She was a follower of Jesus. Her care and character were so different than the nurse before. I told her about the previous conversation I had with the nurse. She was sad to hear about this and thanked me for not adhering to that advice. This lady suggested I get a high-risk doctor just in case something came up. I loved this gal. I pray for her whenever she comes to mind, that our Lord will give her wisdom and strength in helping those she serves. This lady found a doctor that was from Seattle and renowned for her work with high risk pregnancies. That's how God put a special doctor in place for us before we even knew we would need one.

After I got the papers I needed, and the doctor assigned, Paul took me to the doctor's office to get an ultrasound. My momma came along to support us. While I lay on the table in the ultrasound room, the technician looked nervously at her screens and said, "Call her doctor please." She glanced over at me with a fake smile and said, "I just want to have someone else look at it too." I knew something was wrong. She wasn't fooling me with her careful words. We had been through enough trauma at that point to notice more of it on the horizon. The workers were trying to be calm, but we could see it all over their faces. My doctor told us sometime afterwards that our baby was under one pound. They could see he was a boy. But, the cushion between baby and "hello world" was only 0.5 centimeters. Why this happened, no one ever really found out. After the ultrasound was over, the technician didn't want me to stand up. They wheeled the bed down the hall where our high-risk baby doctor checked me over. She just happened to be at the clinic that day. She looked at Paul and me and said, "I'm so sorry. We are going to do everything we can." What in the heck did that mean? Our hearts, which were already so heavy, just dropped through the floor. All we could do was cry. We needed a miracle while we were waiting for our son.

Those with an untrained eye for noticing the presence of God could ask where He was in all of this. We knew God was right there. You see, I had been in labor all those days, pushing in the bathrooms of three continents: Africa, Europe, and North America. With all of that, God kept our baby boy alive. He could have easily been born on one of the three planes over a big ocean far from land with no help to save him or me. I could have given birth in the London airport where I spent so much of my time trying to go to the bathroom. He could have been born in the 3rd floor room we were renting at the church in Nairobi. I felt like "something was falling down out of me." Or he could have been born in our rural community of Kenya, where we only had electricity half the time and had well water with red worms. We were witnessing a miracle and we were fully aware of it. Still, we were so scared at the news from the doctor. They sent me straight from the doctor's office to the hospital. There I would stay for the next 2 ½ months, taking a slew of medications and other things to flush my system of whatever my body had experienced in Africa. They tilted my bed so my feet were way higher than my head, to let gravity help keep our son inside. I was on total bed rest. I had been under such stress in Kenya before we left that my body couldn't handle it anymore.

Everyone in my medical team and family spent the next few months doing everything they could to make our stay at the hospital as pleasant and calm as possible. It was hard to be calm when we had just left our other two children behind. We were homeless. Paul had a job, but it was just part time, doing some substitute teaching. We were so depressed. Yet, we were in the middle of a miracle. We knew it; it was happening every day. The doctors believed that our son would be born the day we arrived at the hospital and would probably die. We didn't believe that, but were so broken. It was hard to have any perspective other than grief. My mother, full of faith, made a big sign and put it on our wall. It said, "Baby Boy Coming in July!" It was early April. This did not sound possible. Then she made an enormous calendar, tapped it to our hospital room wall, and would count down the days each day until the due date. Every day, after she got off work, she would come to the hospital and talk to my son in the womb and tell him that he needed to stay inside until July. She was so consistent with these things, the calendar countdown, the announcing to everyone that came into the room that the baby wasn't coming until July, it became very clear that she was holding up faith for us. We didn't have it in us to move in that sort of faith. Part of our miracle was having someone in our lives at that time who boldly professed what our hearts couldn't. It really carried us through those weeks and months. The miracle of faith through my momma was keeping hope alive.

We were at a Catholic hospital and their service to us was so precious. They sent Christian ministers to sit with us daily and pray with us. They had a harp player come and she composed a song to our son. We had therapy dogs come and play with me. Our nephew's class at his Christian school brought gifts and cards. Our home church sent people who sat with us and prayed with us. All these things meant so much to us. We were overwhelmed with love through the ministry of compassion from others. We would not have made it through emotionally without it. We saw the face of God through so many people, not just our parents, siblings, and friends. People who simply heard about our story gave of their time and love towards us. This was a miracle. It was what we genuinely needed at that time to continue to stay focused. We didn't take it for granted. We were waiting in a season of miracles; not the kind of miracles where the blind see and the lame walk, but the kind where despair is displaced by hope and every day that your baby lives is a celebration, not just for you, but for those around you. These were our days of waiting for our son to be born.

To keep watch on how he was developing and to know what they had to deal with concerning a premature birth, they took me down for an ultrasound about three times a week. This gave Paul and me an opportunity to get to know our son in the womb very well. He was always jumping in there. He loved to move. While in the hospital, he put on some good weight. He loved to pat his feet up and down in the birth canal. This was not so great for keeping him inside, but it really showed his personality. He would turn his face to look towards the light in the womb and he loved to listen to music. He was so excitable. We worked hard to keep him calm. Paul and I decided to look up the name from the dream I had before we went to Kenya. In that dream, I dreamed about a man named Josiah who was my son. We found out that Josiah means "Fire of God". And, after some prayer, we decided that our son would be called Josiah. We told the harpist that came to play for him, and she sang his name through her song. Josiah loved it. He calmed down and rested during the whole harp concert. Though the circumstances were not ideal, we loved the opportunity to get to know Josiah so well through ultrasounds and watching him so closely. It was a miracle of intimacy that the Lord gave us with him. We were so blessed to feel so connected to him in this way.

We had some good missionary friends in Kenya who helped us with our daughter during this time. We were very grateful to them. We felt so helpless as to what we could do for ourselves, so thinking about how to help our daughter, whom we left in Kenya, was even more of a helpless situation. However, God provided each day through the kindness of others for her while we were adjusting to how we would be raising her over the next many years. It was so different than what we had planned, and yet we were so grateful to just be in the story of her life. We wanted children, and God was bringing forth our family in His own unique way. We stayed at the hospital for 2 ½ months. Then they released me to bed rest at home. We went to live at my mom's in her basement. She shared her home, food, and daily help with me while Paul worked. It was a perfect place for us, as we needed a lot of help during that first year back from Kenya. Paul's parents had helped us tremendously while we were in Kenya providing most of our monthly finances, especially in the last couple months. Upon returning, they continued to give us insurmountable emotional support which was indispensable. Life was so fragile for us at that time. We trusted God completely, but we were hurting. We knew God was always good. We saw His goodness in the pain every day.

We spent the rest of the time at home resting. Eventually, we approached Josiah's due date in July. It was a miracle. Our wait for his birth was coming to an end. Josiah decided he was way too comfortable and calm at this point and just passed up his due date. The doctor decided to induce at around 41 weeks. We planned the date. He still hadn't turned yet in the womb, so our doctor made plans for that. However, at the last minute, he turned his head down. We were honored to have my mother-in-law and my mom there at the birth. Paul and I were so happy. The rejoicing was great in our home, as well as in the homes of our extended family and friends. We were still in a season of sadness and were still grieving the loss of our son Michael to a broken adoption system, and having to leave our daughter behind in East Africa. We almost lost our son Josiah, but God saved him and allowed us the gift of raising him. Laughter and joy arose from the ashes of our crisis. Heaven was so near to us in our pain. So near was God, that we could taste the goodness of His love for us. Tears of gratitude washed through our desert and hope grew in the soil of our hearts. We were so blessed! Our son lived! Yet, we still would have praised God had he not. We recognized the beauty of the opportunity we had to get to know Josiah so well just in the womb. We were full of gratitude. What a miracle time this was!

We learned so much about grace, compassion, and intimacy during that waiting season of our lives. Many times, when I was first put in the hospital after arriving from Africa, it really was just Jesus and me. They had me on some serious medications. The Magnesium Sulphate really clouded my ability to connect with the outside world. When people would talk to me, they just sounded like Charlie Brown teachers. My brain couldn't process outside words or conversations. I would just listen to Jesus and talk to Him. I felt so alone in one sense, even in a room full of family and friends at the hospital. At the same time, I didn't feel alone. I knew God was holding me. I felt his love wrapped around me. I can remember telling Jesus that even if I lost everything, what I wanted most was Him. Before they took me off those strong medications, I made a marker in my soul for that quiet alone time I had with Yeshua. I like to go there to that place from time to time. It keeps me anchored. In any waiting season I have been in since then, I know that God has goodness and love for me. I know that I can hide away in that secret place and I can just be with Him. I know that while I am waiting through whatever storm or season, I should look for the miracles. They are always there. God is always there.

Nuclear Sun

"See, I am doing a new thing! Now it springs up; do you not perceive it? I am making a way in the wilderness and streams in the wasteland." (Isaiah 43:19, NIV)

"For we are God's masterpiece. He has created us anew in Christ Jesus, so we can do the good things he planned for us long ago." (Ephesians 2:10, NLT)

Several years ago, when my husband and I lived in Washington, we both were given confirmation from God that we were going to move. God commenced to show us signs and we began to experience changes in our lives that established those signs. At that point, we were still living with my mom since returning from Kenya. We were living in a room in her basement with all our possessions and a small child. We were grateful, but also yearned for space. God was training us in that season to wait with joy. We were in a routine that was dependable and, at times, perhaps monotonous. We had begun to outgrow the space we were so blessed to have at my mom's, and it was time to get our own place where God was sending us. She knew it as well and began to adjust in her heart to the idea that we would eventually leave. This would be a great transition for her. Afterall, she had a front row seat to seeing her grandchild grow up. Paul and I began to pray about the location of where we were being guided to move. We looked all over Washington for affordable housing. Little did we realize at the time, but God wanted to do something fresh in our lives. We were granted several dreams giving us direction and affirmation as to what to expect and what to prepare for. When God gives you a plan, He always provides for it. This is something we have seen over and over. Here are a few of the dreams that were given to me during this season.

I had a dream where we were at our church in Washington. A choir was singing in the sanctuary and Paul and I were in a side room listening to the choir, making little boats out of paper. We began to put our gifts into the boats. Next, we packed them up in a larger box to carry them all. An angel appeared and led us out of the church through a side door in the night. Instantly, our children, Paul and I began to fly in the air and went to a small city I didn't recognize. As the morning hours approached and the sun started to rise, we flew towards a clock tower in this city. And though it was not full light yet, I could see that one of my friends was there hovering above the clock tower. I had no idea who the friend was because her facial features were obscure. But there she was, floating over the clock tower with suitcases in her hand. We saw each other and were excited to connect. As I tried to get closer to her, she flew away. Then the angel took us towards a different area of the city where a small body of water was; it was sort of like a pond or small lake. There was a building not too far from this small body of water. In the background there were brown and sand colored buildings that surrounded this area. There was sand in many places on the ground as well. There were also palm trees scattered around, and there was open land with grass near it, like a large, green space. The angel had us land on a bigger boat in this pond. I saw the building nearby and understood we were to take our little boats with our gifts there to that building. I knew each boat was assigned to someone or something at the building. Then I woke up.

I shared all the details of this dream with Paul. I described it to him as best as I could. We really had no context for how to look anything up. Paul and I, being very familiar with living in Africa, thought that maybe the Lord was showing us that we would move back to Africa, perhaps Egypt. To some, this could seem kind of out there, but for us anywhere God wanted to take us seemed standard protocol. Later, this dream was revealed to us very clearly.

We still weren't in a good financial place to buy a home, so we were simply looking at cheap rentals. Paul had a job teaching math at the local college as an adjunct, so we were focusing our home search in areas that were within driving distance of the school. We searched for months, yet everything seemed to be out of the ballpark as far as our budget was concerned. Around this time, I got a prophetic word in scripture from someone I was not friends with and did not know. It was Isaiah 43:19 which says, "See, I am doing a new thing! Now it springs up; do you not perceive it? I am making a way in the wilderness and streams in the wasteland." This Word gave confirmation to that dream about the clock tower and the pond that we were probably being sent to a desert environment. We still thought it was Egypt, or something like that, at the time. We weren't sure, and we wanted clarity. One day, we asked my mom to keep our son and we drove to a hardware store near Paul's job to pick up a few nuts and bolts for our small business we had on the side. After we left the store, Paul and I sat in our car and prayed. We had brought our prayer tablet with us and listed everything we would have wanted in a home. We asked Yeshua to take our list, add and subtract what He desired, and to show us where he wanted us to move. Paul finished the prayer and we drove home.

About a week later, I had a dream or vision. I'm not sure which one it was, because I was sitting on the couch in our room at my mom's, and Paul was at the computer in front of me working on a motor controller design. I could have fallen asleep, or maybe I didn't, but it doesn't matter. I was suddenly taken up out of myself and outside the house and flew into a different place. I was with Jesus; He was holding my left hand leading me to a place where the sky was so blue, and the sun was so hot it felt like a nuclear bomb had just blown up. We flew high in the sky as the heat was literally scorching my skin in this place. We flew over larger boulders and interesting colorful rock and mountain formations. I noticed the landscape was all desert and there were cacti and lots of open desert land. Out in the middle of this desert was a very large warehouse building that reminded me of a hardware store. The Lord, who was holding my hand, flew me lower toward the building. This place had a sign on it. It was the message I was meant to take away from this adventure under the nuclear sun. The sign was constructed of large capital letters shaped like car-sized blocks on top of the building that said, "W SKY, THE PLACE WHERE ALL YOUR HOUSING NEEDS ARE MET." Jesus didn't say anything about the statement, we just flew up and over towards the main road next to that building. Up until that point, I had not seen one car, house, animal, or person. Unexpectedly, a car was driving down that road. My eyes somehow zoomed in very close to see the license plate on the car. It had no numbers on it. This license plate shown only a picture of a yellow or gold star, with blue at the bottom half and red and yellow rays coming from the top half. There was more to this dream or vision, but this was the meat of it.

I was instantly dropped back into my body, at least that's what it felt like to me, and I was fully aware of everything that had just happened. Paul is very used to these sorts of things in our home. Thus, when I interrupted his work to tell him that the Lord showed me something, he was very interested to hear about it. I told him the whole experience. He quickly looked up on the computer "W Sky." What popped up first was a house in Maricopa, Arizona that had just been sold. The house had been so cheap to buy, and yet was beautiful. And when Paul looked up the state flag of Arizona, it was as I had seen. We knew God had answered our prayer about where we should move. Now we faced a new challenge. We still couldn't buy a home, no matter how cheap they were, so we went to the bank to find out what it would take for us to ready ourselves for such an endeavor. During this time, the Lord gave me many dreams showing me the details of how we would get to where we were headed.

I should mention that I tend to have, what I like to call, "twofer dreams." It's a dream where God shows me something about me and my family that is to come to pass in the future and, in the same dream, He shows me something about someone else that is about to happen or is going on in their lives in the present. When I wake up from these twofer dreams, within a few days or even a few hours, I will get a call, an email, or a text confirming the information God has told me about the other person. That confirmation lets me know without doubt, that everything the Lord spoke to me about my life is coming to pass and that I should pray and prepare. I tend not to share the twofer part of my dreams with others, as they often contain personal information about other people. In fact, unless Holy Spirit makes it very clear that I am to share it with the person it's about, I don't share it with them. God shows me things often about others, but I know He's showing me those things to pray for them. I had many dreams of these kinds during our season of trying to plan for our move to Arizona.

Some of these dreams really stood out to me and foretold many things about the move and what it would be like there. One of my favorite dreams was when my family and I were in a house in the desert. This house had a well that drinking water comes from. The well had a blue light above it. It reminded me of a blue light special at a store. Then I noticed cars, many of them coming down a long, dirt road to this house. They were drawn by the light above the well. They had come to drink from the well. Paul and I, and some of my friends were inside the house. Toby Mac was there in the house and began to sing. Toby Mac is the face that the Lord will use sometimes with me when He is showing me important things. When He uses the likeness of Toby, it is always often about ministry, and I always know I need to pay close attention to the details.

The words of the song caused everyone in the house to become excited and hope filled. Everyone was so full of joy, and I opened the front door and began to invite in the people who came to drink from our well. In another dream, the house was blue and there were railroad tracks near it. Toby Mac was moving his headquarters there and we were part of the move. The house had a huge warehouse on the property with big garage doors. I watched Toby Mac and his crew develop the property from the window of the house. The house had a red light at the front door. I walked out to the front of the house and took out an old-school 35-millimeter camera and took a picture of the house and the work that was being done. It was late afternoon, and I saw that a train was making its way down the tracks. The train car said, "Union." Then I woke up.

I also had a dream where I was at the same house in the desert, but it was a school. It was daytime and I could see the hills and mountains that surrounded this property very clearly. It was at least an acre and there was open land all around it. This dream had a lot going on, but I will say that the school was like my Christian school I went to as a kid, and Paul and I were students there. The headmaster of the school lived on the property in a cabin in the back. Water surrounded the cabin. This was significant to me because when I was first entering my journey of healing, God would take me to be with him in a cabin high in a mountainous place. Therefore, I knew the headmaster was Him. In this dream, I would go to His cabin behind the house that was a school and I would learn from Him.

He taught me how fight and defeat the enemy. He was also teaching me specifically how to identify the works of the enemy. It was a unique and specific training I was getting there. In yet another dream in the same home, I was shown RVs parked on the property of the home and the people who owned the RVs being ministered to by Yeshua through us on this land. I also specifically saw a little girl who was Asian, who's family was so blessed by being there that she ran to me in the dream crying. She and her mother were praising God in the dream. It would be years before I would know who that family was going to be. I had several variations of a dream where the land this desert house was on had an ocean next to it. People would come wearing red swimsuits to dip in the ocean on this land.

I had another interesting stand out dream in September of that year about moving to Arizona. In the dream, we were supposed to be packing, but were not quite packed yet. My mom came with a large van and said, "You need to get ready. It's almost time to go." Let me explain. It wasn't really my mom in the dream. It was Holy Spirit. Holy Spirit without fail, always appears to me in dreams using my mom's face, but everything else about her is different. It has been this way for me since my college years. I asked my "mom" what time it was, and Paul and I were shown a clock. This clock had numbers and Hebrew writing. Suddenly, I noticed some friends in the dream. The dream also incorporated some other prophetic things about two dear friends of mine. It was a twofer. I heard someone tell me to get packing again because the time was nearing for us to leave. I asked what time it was again and was shown the same clock, which now had a different time. This scenario was repeated a few more times like this until the dream was over. The twofer part of my dream was confirmed within the next few days. And, though I didn't understand it at the time, those numbers and symbols on that clock told us exactly to the day, and even the hour, when we would drive up to our future home which we hadn't even started looking for yet. I didn't pick up on that part of the dream until after we moved. God was preparing us for what He had planned for us. He was letting us know so that we could ready ourselves.

When the Lord wants to do something new in your life, He always sends you a message through signs and changes in your personal ecosystem. Linda, my mother-in-law, used to tell me that "when you comprehend that God is preparing you for something, He starts giving you opportunities to grow. Therefore, do everything in your power to learn from it and equip yourself with faith for what's ahead. Because when the Lord is ready to act, you've gotta be ready to move." That is the most significant thing she ever said to me about my future. I remember where I was sitting when she said it. I have thought about that conversation many times.

I want you to be encouraged, loved ones. Be encouraged when you are in seemingly monotonous seasons of life, or in transitional seasons. They don't last forever. Everything on earth eventually comes to an end. Use your time to increase whatever good can be increased, and grow in every way possible in the Word. God allows us circumstances to help us prepare for the journeys before us. He gives us rays of light in our moments of uncertainty. He gives us peace for the crossing ahead. If you have been given a dream, literally or figuratively speaking, and it feels too big, then pray for confirmation, because it's probably from the Lord. He always gives us dreams that are bigger than our ability to accomplish them. That way, He gets all the credit. You can never go wrong trusting God.

Let's Celebrate!

"My frame was not hidden from you when I
was made in the secret place, when I was woven
together in the depths of the earth. Your eyes
saw my unformed body; all the days ordained
for me were written in your book before one
of them came to be. How precious to me are
your thoughts, God! How vast is the sum
of them! Were I to count them, they would
outnumber the grains of sand—when I awake,
I am still with you." (Psalm 139:15-18, NIV)

"For this is what the LORD says: …For I know
the plans I have for you"—this is the LORD's
declaration—"plans for your welfare, not for
disaster, to give you a future and a hope. You
will call to Me and come and pray to Me,
and I will listen to you…—this is the LORD's
declaration…" (Jerimiah 29:10-14, HCSB)

The early morning hours of March 25, 2011 were the moments when our youngest son arrived. And what a commencement it was. Earlier that week, Paul had a business trip to Oregon. As it turns out, the location was about an hour from where one of my closest friends from college lived. For that reason, instead of my husband going alone, we all hopped in the car and took the drive together. Trips like these are always full of thrills and interesting adventures, especially when we are going to see a faithful friend. We got to her house late at night earlier in that week and they hosted us upstairs in their daughter's room, which had a bunk bed set. That meant that I would sleep in the bottom bunk while my husband and older son slept in the top bunk. They have a beautiful home that they built with their own hands, and it was built not just to house family, but to welcome guests. My friend is a doctor, a natural doctor. She has helped my family over the years with many health questions and concerns. She and I met in college in Newberg. Paul and I always have appreciated her and her husband's devotion to God, each other, and their children. Staying there and having time to connect with them was a joyful opportunity.

Paul went to work the next morning and I spent the day with our older son and my friend and her children. We did a few outings and had some great days catching up and sharing good memories. Being old college friends meant we had a lot to talk about. Our family has always enjoyed our time with their family and no matter the distance or the passing of time, we always pick up where we left off. We resumed what we do best when we hang out with each other. We have fun swapping stories, process our life events, and talk about the goodness of God. I wasn't expecting too much more to happen during our time there, so by the time my husband Paul came home and my son and I were getting ready for bed on the night of March 24th, I truly thought the remaining events of our time there would be about the same. Boy was I wrong.

Early in the wee hours of the 25th, before it was time for Paul to get up for work, a visitor stopped by. A man appeared suddenly in the bedroom. He was brilliant and in a bright light, dressed in a rather fancy looking business suit and tie set. He had dark hair and I stood before him. Though I had never seen him before, I knew he was a messenger from God and I also knew that this message was of great importance. I looked next to me and saw a silhouette of my husband, but I also knew he was asleep in real life. Because of his silhouette, I understood that the message was for both of us. The angel said these exact words, "Good News! We're having a baby! Congratulations!" I fully understood that this angel wasn't having a baby. In addition, this one was working as a messenger; I knew it was God saying life was created and something new was about to be birthed. I assumed that must be something other than an actual human.

Whatever my understanding was, I felt the certainty of this message from God that something came alive that moment. The message was unwrapped to me by the angel with all the emotions and faith that I needed to trust that word. I'm not sure what other people have experienced with messages from God, but when I get a message, it's not just the words that are imparted to me. It is the full enchilada of emotions, feelings, thoughts, and intentions that come with the message. It is also the confidence and supernatural impartation of faith I get to trust and wait for the revelation. This message, was packed with a lot of punch. I was so excited, and the excitement began as the words were coming into me.

By the time all the words, "We're having a baby! Congratulations!" came out, I was so overwhelmed with joy! That's a lot of excitement, but that wasn't all. Next, the angel showed me a planner with a calendar in it. He pointed to the date December 15th or 16th, 2011 (reading numbers and words in dreams and visions is always an interesting experience for me) and said, "This is the birth." Then the angel flipped the pages of the planner back to September and pointed to the middle of the month and said nothing. As I was looking at him point to the center of the month, he suddenly closed the book. I instantly noticed it was a black book. The book disappeared and unexpectedly there was a host of people and light beings behind him at a feasting table that was covered end-to-end with food. Some human faces I recognized, others I didn't. The angel spread out his arms with a huge smile on his face and said, "Let's celebrate!" Instantly, the room was dark again, the angel could no longer be seen, and the host of other people, and the feasting table was gone. I sat on the bottom bunk wondering if it was a dream or if I really was awake the whole time. It really didn't matter. The message was from God.

I was so excited to tell my husband, but I figured that this could wait until he got up in a few hours. I couldn't sleep the rest of the night from feeling so excited. When my husband finally awoke, I told him right away all about it. I presumed, since I didn't think I was pregnant, that God was letting us know about something else big that had been given life in our family. Maybe there would be a new business venture or direction. My husband suggested that we should write it down, as we do most visions, dreams, and encounters I receive. I agreed and he went to work while I set out to spend the day with my friend. That evening, after Paul got back from work, we were all sitting around in the kitchen with my friend. I hadn't told her about the encounter I had in her home yet. But she said to me that she had a strong impression from God that I needed some extra nutritional help for my body. Right then and there, she went into her medicine cabinet and took out Vitamins D, B12, folic Acid, and some other stuff. She said to me that she believed that our Heavenly Father spoke to her through an impression about me and my health that I need to take those things for a while. Because I trust the way Holy Spirit leads this friend in her medical practice, I started taking the pills that very night. She gave me extra to take home with me. I did not tell my friend about that encounter I had during that trip. I typically don't tell people things like that unless it's about them, but I think if I had, she would have found it very interesting.

We completed the rest of the day there and had an abundantly peaceful time. When we left to go back home, I went with my vitamins and the excitement of things to come. I had another dramatic dream. It was sometime around the night of the 26th and the morning of the 27th of April, 2011. I dreamed that I was walking down a very wide hallway with some little person whose hand I was holding. Many people around this place were wearing Easter Sunday hats and suits and they were all walking in the same general direction. I was walking in the same direction as the others and noticed that there was a church down the way. I understood in the dream that something big was going to be celebrated at the church soon. The little person who walked with me was so little and so frail. The little person was covered from head to toe in a white covering like a long white dress that went down to the floor. I could not see the little person's face. The little person walked like a crippled old lady, and I fully understood that I was responsible for taking care of this person. I understood that their full care was in my hands. And so, I walked slowly and took my time so that this little person could keep up, even though everyone else around seemed to be moving at a much faster pace.

I was very tired in this dream, but knew I could not shirk my duty of caring for this person. However, I wanted to take a short rest on my walk. I saw a bench against one side of the wall and sat there with the little person. Across on the other side of this very wide hallway, right in front of me, was a series of large posters depicting the Passion Week, the week that Jesus was crucified and rose again. I thought to myself, "Oh, this must be Passover Week, Easter! Everyone else must be headed to church. I'll take this little person and we'll go to church as well." I got up to start walking toward the church. As soon as I got up, there was a man in a white suit who I recognized as Jesus. There was also a giant-sized really bright guy, maybe as much as nine feet tall, made of pure light that walked right up to me. I knew it was a messenger. He said these words, "What a precious gift you've been given. What a precious gift. Take care of it." Then he seemed to give a bighearted smile to the little person I had with me. Jesus did as well. They both had their eyes on the little person.

Later in that month I became rather ill, though I didn't think I was pregnant, I went to the doctor just to get a general checkup. The doctor who saw me asked if I thought I was pregnant. I said no. She suggested I get a pregnancy exam done and I told her that I really didn't need to. I said I wasn't the most fertile gal on the planet, and I didn't use birth control and only managed to give birth once in all my years of marriage. The doctor then said to me, "Well that's good. It's fine not to use birth control. If you get pregnant, all you have to do is have an abortion. I always encourage women to do that anyway." I was almost speechless. Almost, but not quite. I replied, "I would never kill my baby." To that response, she turned around and starting writing something in the notes and told me I was done. This was the second time in my life that a doctor or nurse suggested to me that I should have an abortion as the natural course of action to being pregnant.

I made a mental note that if I ever was pregnant again, I would not have that person as my doctor. That appointment was a very important one for me, because it gave me a lot to ponder. I have come to understand more clearly that many girls do not know how valuable they are. Thus, they cannot perceive the value of others. I think that many women who have abortions do not even realize that they have ended the earthly life of a living human being. These girls are often pressured into it and are led to embrace lies about who is growing inside them. Sometimes, well-meaning, influential people who are really wanting to help women, will paint a picture of them doing something noble for society by having an abortion. Our industrialized nations place a high priority on convenience. People's desire to access that convenience has taken precedent over the right of life for those who don't have a voice. I imagine that many women who seek identity in accomplishments would agree with that doctor. Many women who have unwanted pregnancies from undesirable circumstances would also agree with that doctor. But I know that heaven is crying out for those that can't speak for themselves. I know that God is Love and is full of abundant grace and unending forgiveness for all those mamas who come to realize their motherhood, even after their babies are in heaven. Equally so, I know that heaven is calling out to all the well-meaning family, friends, and doctors that encourage the death of the unborn. I count that visit to that doctor as important because it sparked a fire in me to pray for women around the world to realize how great the love of God is for them, born and unborn.

As the weeks progressed, I wondered what great thing was going to be "birthed" into my family after that encounter with the Lord. As you are reading this, surely it is obvious to you what God was speaking. But as it was for us, pregnancy was the last thing on earth we believed had happened. I waited with anticipation to see the revelation of all that was spoken to us.

My sickness only got worse as time went by. Eventually, Paul said we should get a pregnancy test just to cross it off the list. I stayed home and he went and picked one up for us. It was positive! By the way, this was the week of Passover that year! We were astonished at the test results. We booked an appointment with a different doctor than the one I saw last time. My husband and I got my mom to watch our older son while we went to our appointment. The doctor did all the standard exams, and then told us that the due date was December 16, 2011. Paul and I looked at each other and smiled. God really is amazing. It turns out that the estimated conception date for the baby I was carrying fell around March 24/25, 2011. Wow! On the day God breathed life into our child and placed him in my womb, He saw fit to announce our son's existence. In addition, He invited us to celebrate our baby's life at the very beginning. I believe that heaven always celebrates every person from conception.

My prayer is that we begin to celebrate with God the life of the unborn. No one is a mistake. We have all been given the precious gift of life. We are designed to need each other, and we need Him. We are loved. Even in the context of very difficult circumstances, all babies are a new beginning for the family they are born into. Unborn children are like a message of love from our Heavenly Father. They are a call for us to become more loving, less selfish, more like Jesus. Psalm 139 is one of the love letters in scripture that speaks the heart of our Creator towards us. We are of infinite worth at every stage of our life.

There is so much more I can tell you, the joy of telling everyone about our baby on the way, the goodness of God throughout the pregnancy. Not only did we celebrate, but we welcomed others to do so as well. We would share what God was doing in our lives with our family, friends, and even strangers. I can remember telling a fellow parent of our son's Children Bible Study club one Wednesday night about the angelic encounter and how we just found out the revelation of it through the pregnancy test. I didn't know her personally, but she remembered my story and shared it with others. When I would randomly see her, she would excitedly ask me how the pregnancy was going. We wanted anyone who wanted to applaud the goodness of God to join in with our praise. It was a fabulous season to be in. My pregnancy went smoothly all the way through. This was in great contrast to the process we went through with Josiah. My youngest son's birthing story is beautiful. As birthing a child tends to go, it was indeed a very exciting event that wasn't without adventure.

Oh! I absolutely must tell you what happened in the middle of September 2011. Remember, the angel pointed at two dates in the calendar. Our small home business, which typically made only side money at that time, made many thousands of dollars in the month of August and the first half of September 2011. As a result, all our debts (except for student loans) went to zero on September 14th. This was WAY earlier than we had ever thought possible. We had no more credit cards. No more car loan. No more lines of credit. This put us in the financial position to do the other assignment that God had given us, which was to move to Arizona. It was amazing how much God did for us and through us. Everything from the personal message from Him, to Holy Spirit guiding my doctor friend in Oregon to prophetically treat me based on the needs of a pregnant woman. Everything God did during those nine months was so packed with meaning and purpose for us and those around us. That is why those early morning hours of March 25, 2011 will forever be burned into my heart as the day that our youngest son came into the world, bringing with him the abundance from the Creator's heart.

> "My frame was not hidden from you when
> I was made in the secret place, when I
> was woven together in the depths of the
> earth…" (Psalm 139:15-18, NIV)

Here He Comes!

"Or what woman who has 10 silver coins, if
she loses one coin, does not light a lamp, sweep
the house, and search carefully until she finds
it? When she finds it, she calls her women
friends and neighbors together, saying, 'Rejoice
with me, because I have found the silver coin
I lost!' I tell you, in the same way, there is
joy in the presence of God's angels over one
sinner who repents." (Luke 15:8-10, HCSB)

"See what great love the Father has lavished
on us, that we should be called children of
God! And that is what we are! The reason
the world does not know us is that it did
not know him." (1 John 3:1, NIV)

It came in sudden waves of pain. I knew it was time. The spacing of
the timing between each one, and the calm between them, told me
that he was coming out soon. It was December 16, 2011. Right on
schedule. I found myself tracking the closing gap of time between
the pain and the peace times of this process of labor. Paul and I were
ecstatically anticipating this day, and after such a beautiful and dramatic announcement of it, we felt as ready as we could be. But like
most things in our lives, this wasn't going to be an average birthing
experience.

I told my Mom that my contractions were getting really close
and really intense and that Paul and I were going to make plans to
head out to the hospital. We also had planned for my Mom to take

care of our other son while we went. My mama had other plans that evening. She said that she was on her way to drive to Oregon to pick up my youngest brother that night. Anyone who knows my momma knows that when she sets her mind to a plan, she doesn't stray from it too much. Convincing her that I was close to delivering our baby was difficult. She used her "mom doc" skills, looked me over head to toe, and said, "You're fine. That baby isn't coming out until I get back. I've got to go get your brother. Hey, will you and Paul watch the kids for me while I'm gone?" Of course, the question wasn't really a question. It was more of a statement. She was getting her keys and heading towards the garage door as she asked it.

As the garage door was closing and my mom was driving away, Paul and I considered the fact that we had all of my foster siblings in the house with us, Josiah, and the two of us. Our little five-person car wasn't going to cut it for driving me and all the children to the hospital if those contractions got any closer. We did what we always do when we are faced with a moment like this. We prayed. It was a simple prayer. We asked Jesus if He would slow the contractions and hold off John's birth until my Mom returned. Perhaps, my mom had prayed the same thing. I have found through the years of getting to know my mother that sometimes her statements are really the product of an internal process of prayer and faith in action. I believe my mom telling me "You're fine. That baby isn't coming out until I get back" was most likely an example of that. There we were, trusting that God would answer our prayer to hold off the contractions for the next several hours.

John was a calm child in the womb most of the time. He loved to relax and typically only got excited if his brother Josiah was making lots of noise around him. Oh, I remember the way he would press his little bottom against my belly. He was a big baby, and we knew it. We did not choose his name. It was chosen for him by God. Here is how we came to know his name: One night, when I was very ill in bed earlier in the pregnancy, in a lot of pain, possibly from M.S. symptoms, one of John's angels made himself visible to me. He sat next to me in the bed, full of light, but with human facial features. He appeared with dark brown, wavy hair, and he wore a long sleeve gown that went down below his feet. He had a wooden bowl in his hand and a wooden spoon. Inside the bowl, was a translucent shimmering soup-like mixture that seemed to be almost alive. He began to feed me this soup, spooning it into my mouth. Between each spoonful, and as I would feel the wealth of it and its goodness going down through me, the angel would rub my pregnant belly. While rubbing and smiling at my belly, as if he could see inside, he would say, "John" in a language that I didn't fully know, but it was clear that it was John in English. It may not make sense reading this, but that's how it was. The angel repeated this feeding me the soup and talking to my baby calling him "John." He also said other things to him in that language I didn't understand fully, but I knew my baby's name now. It was obviously John. Thus, when I was able to talk to Paul about it in the next few hours, we agreed that we would call our son what Heaven was clearly calling him.

And on the evening my mom went to Oregon to get my brother, it was evident that John was wanting to come out! I was trusting God to answer our prayer to stave off the contractions, and hold them off He did. Over the next two hours, my contractions began to get further apart. Eventually, they stopped all together. I wasn't even feeling the normal discomfort that sometimes comes during the end of the last term of carrying a baby. It was such a calm sensation I had over me. I began to wonder if he would maybe be born several days late. I decided to play Mario Brothers with our other son Josiah and had a great evening laughing at my husband's jokes. We went to bed and were doing fine. No birth on the horizon that night! Or so it seemed...

At about 2:15 in the morning, the garage door opened, and my mom and brother rolled in, back from Oregon! Since I heard them arriving, I got up to meet them in the hallway. As soon as my brother walked into the hallway from the garage and said hi to me, I felt the most excruciatingly painful contraction. It hit me like a freight train. As my Mom was walking up the stairs, I felt like I was about to die. As she went up to her room, she looked pleased that I had not given birth yet and simply told me to let her know when we wanted her to keep Josiah. I went to our room and laid across the bed. Paul could clearly see this was a major contraction. We were trying to track it, but it was hard because I felt like there wasn't any real spaces of calm. The time between contractions was almost zero. Paul called the nurse to ask when it was appropriate to come into the hospital. She said, "What are you doing on the phone right now? Get her to the hospital NOW!" I couldn't talk really at this point. It felt like my mind was blowing up every few seconds. We told my mom, and she came down to wake our son Josiah and get him dressed while Paul and I went on. In the hallway, my water broke. I had this plan of giving birth naturally, and at that point the pain was so crazy I declared out loud, "I changed my mind! I don't want a natural birth!" Sorry, sister! That ship has sailed!

Paul had done some reading during the pregnancy on how to deliver a baby in case we didn't make it to the hospital. He almost had to use that knowledge, but we made it. I struggled out of the car. They put me in a wheelchair and Paul checked me in. Before they took me to the birthing room, they took me to an assessment room to see how close I really was to delivering. The nurses there insisted I give them a urine sample. I struggled to the bathroom and tried to position the cup in the right location to take the urine sample. I gave them a sample alright, an avalanche of runny poop.

The nurse decided they didn't need a urine sample. She wanted to have a look and see what was going on in the birthing region. The nurse took a peek, smiled, and said to the other Nurse there, "Take her to her birthing room NOW." From there, they pushed the bed I was laying on down the long corridor and to the birthing unit. They informed my doctor that I was ready. As I arrived in the room, so did my mom, Josiah, and my brother. He helped to distract Josiah for us behind a curtain in the birthing room so that my mom could see the birth, and so that Josiah wouldn't freak out. My youngest brother, who had just come from college, stayed home to care for my foster siblings. It was a beautiful sacrifice on their parts which allowed my mom to come to John's birth. I'm sure that's what my mom's prayer was all along when she wanted to pick him up from college. Everything was coming together for the big welcome.

The nurse in the room was trying to get things ready before the doctor arrived. They put me in the position and grabbed the towel, and that's when the doctor walked in. She looked to see how close I was to delivering and told me to start pushing. It all went by very quickly with just a few pushes. "Here he comes!" they said as he came right out. John was born! He came out of the womb just around 4 AM. Oh, what a welcome we gave him! This much anticipated moment was full of tears of joy and lots of picture-taking moments. We wanted to capture everything about that miraculous time in a way we could always go back to it to remember and embrace the love. The smiles all around the room were amazing.

I believe that kind of joy is a shadow of how heaven rejoices when one of us comes into the kingdom of God. I could imagine someone in heaven saying, "Here they come!" as the entourage in heaven erupts in shouts and cries of joy. The scriptures tell us in Luke 15 that there is rejoicing in the angelic presence over new believers. Heaven celebrates when sinners come home to God, not unlike the celebration that God invited us to participate in over our son when He announced him to us. When someone comes into the kingdom of God, tell your friends, tell your neighbors, tell your barber. Bring your joy to the world. It's miracle. Every life is a beautiful miracle. 1 John 3:1 says to embrace the abundant love our Father has lavished on us so that we could be called His children. This is who we are!

Four Horns and a Blizzard

"The LORD is the One who will go before
you. He will be with you; He will not leave
you or forsake you. Do not be afraid or
discouraged." (Deuteronomy 31:8, HCSB)

"God is not a human who lies or a mortal who
changes his mind. When he says something,
he will do it; when he makes a promise, he
will fulfill it." (Numbers 23:19, CJB)

Before moving to Arizona, we received many signs and wonders
from the Lord. The most epic dream I had about moving to our
future home in Maricopa was all about the journey going there. In
this dream, Paul had a large truck with our things and drove in front.
I was in a car with our boys behind him, but I wasn't driving. A tall,
dark man was driving the car. I had no idea who he was in the dream,
but I knew I could trust him. Eventually in the dream we hit very bad
weather. The blizzard developed to such intensity that it reminded
me of that scene from a well-known 1984 movie about a little boy's
adventure reading a story that never ends. In the movie, the hero
of the book must walk through the snowstorm on a journey to the
South to get to an oracle. He places his hands on a blizzard blasted
ice wall that allows him to press through and get to the other side
where it is a calm peaceful night.   Well, that is what happened
in the dream sort of. I was so afraid. The blizzard was so merciless.
We no longer could see Paul or his truck ahead of us. We were freezing in the car. Eventually, we reached a wall of ice before us. The tall
man who was driving got out of the car and placed his cold hands on

the ice wall and began to use all his power to press his way through it. I watched him struggle but eventually the ice wall gave way to a small hole for us to go through. On the other side of it was our house on a big area of land surrounded by beautiful mountains and it had a few palm trees near the house. The sky was blue, and Paul was there with the truck. It was as though the storm never happened.

Once I woke up, I realized we were still in Washington at my mom's house. Over the next season of our life, we worked on all the areas the bank said we needed to work on to be able to qualify for a home loan. We worked hard at saving what we could from Paul's job at the college and the little revenue we got from our home business. Paul is also an engineer, so our online home business is where we sell his engineering designs and products that are used with electric motors, inverters, and other associated things. Our company definitely helped with small bills, but was not able to support us fully. That's why Paul had a job at our local community college teaching math. However, his work as an engineer was growing, and other people and companies were noticing what he had designed. Occasionally Paul would do independent contractor work for people and other companies. One such company wanted him to do some work for them in Oregon. It was on that business trip in March that I got the "We're having a baby!" message that I wrote about earlier.

By the middle of September of that year, all our debts were paid in a way that was out of our control. This put us in the financial position we needed to be in to buy a house. Also, with the night classes Paul was teaching at the college as an adjunct, we were able to save enough money to put 20% down on our future home. I then understood the September date and why it was a black book that the angel closed. Closing the financial books for that year and being in the black. That was the message to us in that.

Now that we had the ability to get a home loan and enough to put down on it, we needed to actually go online and find a house to buy. Sometimes when you know what God has told you to do, you go slowly about it, not because you don't want to obey, but because there are things in your life that you feel you can't leave or figure out. We were in that place. We had no plan for income after moving to

Maricopa, Arizona. We had visited a friend in Phoenix once, but had no connections down there whatsoever. We knew we could take our home business, but that only brought in maybe $500-$1500 per month. Besides Paul and I, our daughter in Kenya, and our son Josiah, we now had baby John. We struggled in our faith in how we were going to make ends meet when we moved. We also saw the sadness our family felt when we talked about moving far away from them. All of this made it easier for us to hesitate on many of the steps God was taking us through towards our big move. I had so many dreams and prophetic words about the move and the details of what the move would look like. Therefore, we were being confirmed all the time about it. God always makes provisions for His plans; all He asks us to do is step into it. During this season, I had to remind myself of that often.

However, it still felt hard to leave a decent paying job and family and go to the unknown. By faith, we decided we should go ahead and start looking for a house. At first, we focused on the houses in the city part of Maricopa. Maricopa was a small town. It was just houses, a few stores, and the John Wayne Highway going right through. The main part of town seemed like the obvious area to search for a home. The Lord allowed every house we were interested in to be outbid by someone else. We weren't sure what to do, until a house popped up on the outskirts of Maricopa. It was still in city limits but in the open desert land near the mountains. The price was just right. It was on an acre and a quarter, and it didn't have an HOA. That's important to us.

Paul asked me how I felt about living away from the city. I told him I preferred that anyway. We prayed about it and decided to place a bid. No one else put a bid on this house. Our realtor there, also a believer, agreed to do all our house inspections and viewings for us. We never went down to personally see it. We trusted that God would bless the eye of our realtor. After an inspection and exchanges with the sellers, we purchased the house. We signed all our papers remotely. They mailed us the key. We owned a house! I called the friend we had visited in Arizona and told her that we were moving to a city called Maricopa. She excitedly told us that she was in the middle of moving back to France and was now staying with a friend from her missionary organization in Maricopa. We had planned to get together before she left, assuming I got there in time.

However, we were still living in Washington. We hadn't made plans to leave yet and still had no plans for work. I had a dream about this time that Paul and I were moving to a western town. As we were loading up our wagon to head out, the Sheriff came up to Paul and said in a cowboy accent, "The boss says you're doing a great job and He's proud of ya. He wants to give you a gift to take with ya on your journey." Instantly we were transported to a barn where a large black bull with four horns stood. Paul, my daughter in Kenya, and our two sons all grabbed on to one horn. I stood in front of them with my 35-millimeter camera. I asked Paul in the dream, "Is this for meat?" He responded, "No, this is for seed." Then I took a picture of each of my family members. Next, we appeared back at the wagon and Paul was hitching the bull to the wagon. We then started on our way. Then I woke up. I knew God was confirming to Paul and me something about our future income, but I didn't have perspective about what was coming up next.

Paul and I set a moving day for ourselves in December, right before Christmas. God enjoys giving me unique and wonderful surprises around Christmas. We made plans to visit some college friends before we left. Before we could begin our journey, our daughter Lynette contracted Malaria and had some other school fee issues that popped up. Our moving and traveling budget was reduced and we were now short around $400. We visited our friends in Oregon anyway. This was the same house where I had the "We're having a baby" dream. While we were there, Paul visited a company that he had done work for. Upon arriving there, he noticed they had built a 3-phase motor. The company explained that they eventually wanted to do a motor controller for it. This was not why he had come. They had just asked him to come so he could drop off a few things he had worked on before we headed to Arizona in the next couple days.

Paul had independently been working on his first version of a 3-phase motor controller and had just stuck it in the trunk of the car, because he thought it was cool, and wanted to show it off to his friends. When they showed him the motor, he told them that he had what they needed in his trunk! I repeat, we had no prior knowledge that they were working on a motor. They asked to see it. He went out to the car and brought it in. He hooked it up, and their motor started spinning! The company offered Paul a full-time engineering job right on the spot. Paul told them that we were moving to Arizona in three days, so he couldn't take it. The boss said to Paul, "No problem." He told Paul he could work from home and that the paycheck would begin in a few weeks. Now we still were short on the moving money, but now we had the income once we got there! It was John's 1st birthday that day. Before we left Oregon, the vice president of the company gave John a birthday card. While driving back to Washington, we opened the card. It was $400 cash inside it. All I could do was cry.

God had provided everything we needed for income. When the last college job check ended, the new check began. We never missed a pay period. We left Washington a few days before Christmas with a heart full of faith. Everything came to pass as God showed us. Paul drove the moving truck and drove ahead of us. We were coordinating our stops together. My younger brother (the middle child), who happens to be much taller than I am, offered to drive my sons and me to Arizona. Before we even left Oregon, my brother got a gut feeling that we should change my windshield wipers. It had started to rain, and he felt that their efficiency could have been better. We had no idea snow was coming in California. Our car had no heating system. For the last several months that didn't matter. It was about to matter soon. We hit one of the worst blizzards I had ever seen going through northern California. It was so bad that trucks and cars were driving off the road and the freeway was littered with cars trapped in the snow. We were freezing, and I had brought no snow clothes for the kids. I used my socks to put over my baby's hands and my brother shared his gloves with my other son. We piled all the traveling clothing on top of them.

My brother's hands were so cold as he drove us less than 5 miles per hour to avoid sliding off the freeway. We stopped at a Subway restaurant to get information about the roads ahead. Paul had already gone on. Lots of truckers and big rigs were stranded there and they were discussing the moving truck that had flipped over on the freeway in the direction we were headed and that they thought the driver was either dead or seriously injured. This news caused me to panic, because Paul had been driving our moving truck. The last time we talked to Paul on the phone, he was telling us not to come that way, then the phone cut out and we couldn't reach him again. I was devastated and went back to my car crying. My brother assured me that the moving truck they spoke of wasn't Paul's. But I knew that no one is exempt from troubles and heartache. I thought about the dream I had about the tall man getting us through the ice wall and how on the other side, Paul was there. That became what I held on to. I trusted that God was truly going to bring my husband to the other side of the ice wall we were in. To add to the stress of it all, it was also Paul's birthday and we were hoping to celebrate over pizza when we met up that night.

Even though I believed that Paul was fine, I just felt like crying. As my brother drove on through the storm at a snail's pace, I just cried. By nightfall, while we were still inching along, the state of California decided to close part of the freeway down. Paul borrowed a phone and called us in Redding, California at a gas station. He told us that they had closed the freeway and to go a different way. However, God had blessed us to pass the portion they closed. We found out we were only a few exits away from where Paul ended up stopping with the moving truck. We met him at the gas station where he was hanging out, right off the freeway. I was so happy! God did it. My brother pressed through the ice storm! Paul was alive and well! We found a hotel for the night. Within walking distance was a pizza parlor. It was a perfect ending to such a stressful day.

The rest of the journey was long, exciting, and way less dangerous. We drove through California, took a left at L.A., and followed the freeway until we ended up on an old highway that took us right to our house. We arrived in Maricopa late at night. Once we got to the part of town we were moving to, we noticed that we had to cross railroad tracks to get to our dirt road. This reminded me of the railroad tracks I had seen in previous dreams about this house. We drove down the dirt road towards our new home. My brother and

Paul unloaded the whole truck that night and then took the truck to the drop-off location in town. They got the job done quick. Then we were able to take out the surprise we had in there for the boys. Paul had put a Douglas Fir Christmas tree in the truck right before we left Washington. The next morning, we saw everything for the first time: our well, the surrounding mountains, the desert cacti and desert plants, the palm trees in front, the blue sky, and the desert in the backyard as far as the eye could see. It was just as we had been shown long before we even started looking for a house there. The next day was December 23rd. Paul drove my brother to the airport so that he could fly back home. I am so grateful that my brother was that tall man in my dream. I am glad that he followed the voice of God in his life and purchased new windshield wipers. He even purchased the best kind. We needed those wipers to get through that storm. I am so glad that God used him to press through the storm for us. It is a trip that all of us will remember.

With my brother back home and my family settling into the beauty of our new home, I walked around the yard and thanked God for all He had done for us. We put up our Christmas tree and spent the day making beautiful decorations to commemorate the journey God had given us. We put some of our artwork on the walls around the tree. Then we looked up on our cell phone what churches were having Christmas Eve services. Because we had spent so much time doing arts and crafts together, most of the church services had already started. But there was one that was going to start in the next hour. It was very dark, and this was clearly a late service. We got dressed, hopped in the car, and put the GPS on to show us how to get there. We couldn't see any details of the outside area of the church, but we could see it was in a school building. The service was beautiful, and we decided to visit there the next Sunday.

The next Sunday, we once again followed the GPS. On the way, we passed an area where there was a clock tower and little shops. I remembered the dream about the clock tower and the unknown friend floating over with her suitcases. I knew my friend who used to live there was the friend in the dream. As we arrived towards the school where the church was, we noticed it was right next door to a park that had a pond that was surrounded in the distance by homes that were all sand colored. There were palm trees and a sports field nearby. I remembered in the dream we were to take our gifts to the church next to all of that. In that very moment, Paul and I knew what community God wanted us to worship with. Everything was just as the Lord said it would be.

There are so many stories I could tell about our time living in Maricopa, so many amazing people we met and love. God provided boldly for the plans He laid forth for us to follow. Paul had worked for that company in Oregon under that agreement for four years. I think of the four horns everyone in my family held while I took a picture of them in the dream. And God really used that job not as meat, but for seed. During those four years, Paul got to try many new designs, and his skills as an engineer grew.

I am so grateful that God is always looking out for my future. If you ever wonder if Jesus cares about your tomorrows, He does. There is not a day of your life that He doesn't know about. He wants to be a part of all your activity. Let him lead you wherever He sees fit. He made you and He understands what's best for you. It's hard to give up what we think is helping us at the time or our good ideas for our future. We had a difficult season of faith trusting that our finances would work out with this move. What we didn't know, was that Holy Spirit had already orchestrated all the people involved with our future work opportunities. All we had to do was show up to receive the gift. When you know that you are called to something, pray and trust Holy Spirit's leading. Just show up, and you will receive.

Sisterhood

"Say to wisdom, 'You are my sister.'
Call understanding your special
friend." (Proverbs 7:4, NLV)

"I thank my God for all the memories I
have of you." (Philippians 1:3, NOG)

Most women know that one of the greatest gifts we have is the strength of our sisterhood. The kinship of women in our lives keeps us balanced, supports us in our goals, and can help us unearth treasures in our difficult journeys. Sisterhood is the backbone of many accomplishments in the world. Some of the most noteworthy women in history drew support and strength in their times of crises from the faithful women in their lives. Why, even Mary, the mother of our Savior had the support of Elizabeth. My family has been enlarged by the women I call friends and sisters. I have many sisters. They come from all over the world. For me, being in a sisterhood with the amazing women in my life that Holy Spirit brought to me has been essential towards helping me move forward daily, growing as a healthy and healed woman of God.

A sisterhood is a community of ladies who in a crisis will join forces, carry you when you are weak, and dig holes in someone else's roof to get you to the feet of Jesus. The birth of my sisterhood began in my early years when I was a little girl. I have a few extremely valuable and irreplaceable friends from my time growing up in Texas. Those ladies were there in some of the worst years of my childhood, and because they were there, I have so many happy memories. They brought joy, adventure, and sometimes a little trouble. There is Pam, my bosom-buddy during the years at my Christian School. There is also Rhonda, who also doubles as my godsister. One time, my dad almost took her home from preschool instead of me because he couldn't tell us apart. Rhonda is one of those friends who I know that I can call anytime. She is a doctor down in Texas, helps to care for her mom, and she is busy at her church. However, she takes the time to remember me in so many ways throughout the year. Rhonda even flew to where we lived to sing at one of the Seders we hosted during Passover. She is one of the oldest friends I have in my sisterhood.

Then of course there is Christie Love, my cousin, who was the very first person to be in my sisterhood. We have known each other since we were babies! She was in my babyhood before it became a sisterhood. To be honest, it was meant to be. We are close in so many ways. Our birthdays are close, our moms are best friends, we saw each other all the time, and we even went to the same church. We have had marvelous adventures together, and I talk to her about planning new ones all the time. One of the most exciting voyages we took together was going to Hungary to visit my very good friend Monika and her family. Christie Love and I took this trip with yet another person in my sisterhood who had just moved to France. Oh, the stories we collected during that rousing adventure. For me, one of the best parts of that complete Euro-adventure was the celebration of Hungary's birthday in Budapest. I can't remember how old the country was turning, but it was a party of massive proportions. We danced in the streets all night with very happy Hungarian strangers. And I love that I got to share that amazing experience with my sisters, my friends.

During my college years, I met many compassionate young ladies and some of those gals have been so stable in my life through all these years that I can call or text them anytime, and we pick up right where we left off. These ladies have become extended family to Paul and me. They have housed us, fed us, supported us in missions, prayed for us in times of crisis, and loved us unfailingly through all seasons. These friends are spread over states and countries, but are all just a phone call, text, or email away. My college roommates were among the first ladies to become close friends with me in college.

They weren't just roommates; they were closer than that. I needed and appreciated the depth of their hearts to me during that time of my life.

My freshman roommate and her family were amazing people who loved God and loved me well that year. During college, I spent Easter with her family. It was an important time in my life. I got to see a healthy family up close. I loved to watch them interact. My sophomore year roommates showed up large in personality and they were like magnets to all the guys on campus. Tam is one of my friends from this time, and she's still such a faithful sister in Christ to me. It was a season filled with fantastic laugh and cry all night binges and fancy-free outings to Shari's Diner, where I would take three hours looking at the menu, only to pick chicken fried steak every time. We had wonderful times at our local drive-in theater in Newberg, OR. Our town also had a historic indoor theater that had seats that rocked back and were covered in old red velvet. The elderly woman who worked the window out front always gave back two-dollar bills for change. How fun it was to go with some of my friends on a Friday night to the theater. Often, we had already seen the movie. I mean, they only had one or two at any given time. We'd just go for the experience we'd have together. I also had grand adventures with Tam on her job helping to sell merchandise for famous Christian singers coming into the area. What a hoot that was. It was like having backstage passes! Once, Bob Carlisle had a terrible sore throat. Finding cough syrup and bringing it to Bob with my friends was fun. I also got some great words of encouragement from Rich Mullins on another occasion.

During my junior and senior year of college, I picked up some amazing friends as well. They became like family to me. We had amazing adventures driving to the ocean, hanging out at the Coffee Cottage, and sitting around just laughing and having fun in our rooms. Sometimes our adventures had craziness written all over it. I can recall such a time when my friend Charmain, Monika, and I decided to take a trip to the San Juan Islands in Washington for the weekend. I had just started a new job doing laundry at a nursing home. However, Charmain always had a way about her that always led her to adventure. We rode up in her car, which was a stick shift, and ended up at a bed and breakfast. It was beautiful getting there and being there. The next day I needed to get back to Oregon for work. We were all having so much fun, Charmain and Monika decided to stay at the bed and breakfast another night and invite a friend. Charmain said I could drive back in her car. I couldn't drive a stick shift. The friend that was coming had an automatic, so she left it parked on the Washington mainland side of the ferry and planned to just walk on the ferry over to San Juan after I arrived to get the keys. I caught the ferry from the San Juan side and boated over to the mainland and got the keys to the car. I drove nonstop from the port of the ferry back to my college and made it before midnight. Did I mention that I hit a very large, antlered deer on the way driving in the fast lane? It was scary. The deer was jumping over the median of the freeway and leapt right in front of me. It filled all the space of the front window. God was gracious to me. I saw it in the rearview mirror twitching as a kept driving. This is the first and only time I ever hit a deer. The irony of it all is that so many other things happened over the next week that I forgot all about hitting that deer for almost a solid month. My friend was trying to figure out why her car didn't work very well anymore. I suggested that maybe it was because I ran over a massive buck. There was never a dull moment with these ladies.

Two friends I met at college have modeled patience and kindness, and even today we love to stop and stay at their family farms. I lived with them both in college, each in different years and so the strands of our hearts are bonded in a special way. Jen and I would love to play old spirituals and songs about picking cotton sunup to sundown during finals week in college. Not only was this historical music, but it tapped into our sentiments of finals week testing. At different occasions, I was able to go with friends to Jen's farm. Tam, another college roommate, drove us there a few times. Christie Love, my cousin, joined us at the farm on another trip. Jen's parents would make the best organic meals before organic was cool. That homegrown beef was amazing! I loved everything about the farm, the llamas, the sheep, the chickens. After I was married, Paul and I even went there for a week just to get away and hang out with Jen.

Once, Jen and I took a friend from Kenya to her first American concert. We went to see a Christian band play at a large venue. We stood in line afterwards to get autographs from the Newsboys. While we waited, our Kenyan friend taught us how to do Kenyan dances. We were so inspired by the dances, that Jen and I both took a West African dance class together on campus sometime later. Talk about fun! It really was a wonderful time of bonding that taught me so much about myself. Jo, the other friend who lived on a different smaller farm, taught me more about patience and self-control than any other friend I have. Jo is an extremely disciplined person, and I have learned how to live a more self-controlled and spiritually disciplined life from her. Jo and I spent countless hours hanging with friends at the Hispanic Friends (Quaker) Church in town and hosting get-togethers for youth in our college apartment. She was very active in ministry and outreach to the Spanish-speaking community. After she returned from Costa Rica, she began to dream in Spanish. I know because we shared a room and she always talked in her sleep. She stopped talking in English and started speaking Spanish in her sleep the rest of the year.

In our apartment we had beehives in our walls. That wall made a constant buzzing sound. Our main sitting couch was leaned against that wall and a large painting was nailed into it. We didn't touch the wall because it was very squishy and you could see the rolling bumps under the paint. We notified the landlord, but she never sent anyone to check it. Over time, we got used to it and didn't worry anymore. One day, a guy was sent out by the landlord to check the smoke detectors. He heard the humming in our living room and asked what it was. Rather nonchalantly, we told him it was the beehives. He went silent and left. A few hours later the landlord called and said that she was sending out a person to check our wall. The man that came to check the walls determined that we had two large and very active hives in that wall. What amazing adventures I had living with these women. I have been encouraged to be a better mom, a more respectful daughter to my mom, and a more devoted daughter to my God.

I need people like that in my life. It's easy just to get comfortable in being who we are without any assessment of ourselves from the out-side. A sisterhood helps me to understand who I am through their eyes. It helps me evaluate my behavior, the intentions and thoughts behind my behavior, and my plan for moving in a direction that is best.

After my college years, I had a very established and strong sis-terhood in place. Through my travels, God has given me friends that I can only call family. Many of these friends come from different walks of life and backgrounds, but all of them are light-bearers for Christ. Take my friend Rosie. She and her husband have a lot of chil-dren and they homeschool, so they are very busy. When the symp-toms of M.S. were at their worst, and I couldn't do very much at all physically besides shuffle from one chair to the next, Rosie would come over to my house, which was way out in the boondocks, and clean my house for me. Not only that, she would organize and deep clean my closet, my bathroom, and my kitchen. God showed me His goodness through her and her family. Then there are my two friends D'vorah and Bee. D'vorah organized many activities for our homeschooling community. I wouldn't have met some of my friends without D'vorah's heart to see community thrive. She really believes in connecting families. Bee, an artist and architect, exemplifies the beauty of motherhood. She passionately loves Jesus, her husband, and her children. Bee knows many heart things about me. Those women have stood by my side in many tough seasons. They have been family to me.

Bible study groups have been one of the best places to make life-long friends. My Bible study sisters have been invaluable to me as solid women in my life. I appreciate their passion for Jesus and tireless service to the body of Christ wherever they are. Friends like Shree and Laura remind me of the importance of compassion in all circumstances. My Bible study sisters have opened their homes and hearts to me and my family. When we've needed food, essential oils, a place to sleep for the night, or a garage to keep our dog in for a time, my Bible study sisters have always been there for me. Some of these women really challenge my thinking. They are my go-to people when I need to make big decisions and I want honest opinions. Two good examples of these types of friends are Sasha and Ari. Both are honest, direct, and they see beyond the boundaries of my words. They will listen to what I have to say and then, like an arrow flying towards its target, they will cut right to the heart of the matter. Sometimes I need to let it all sink in before I can process it, but I find that their perceptions of things we discuss are timely and accurate.

Once, while at the library, I was sitting next to a lovely lady from Taiwan who had brought her children to some library event. I was there with my boys. I struck up a conversation with her about Chinese writing, how many different characters there are, and the difference between Mandarin and traditional Chinese. At the time, my oldest son was taking Chinese at our homeschool co-op, so I was interested to find out a few things. I told her my name and she told me hers. We had a wonderful time chatting while the kids did their thing. Upon leaving the library, Holy Spirit told me to go back and ask this lovely lady if she would come to my oldest son's birthday party. I gave her my phone number and address. She came to the party and brought her family. At the party, Holy Spirit told me to ask her to come and share her testimony and a little about her culture at a get together at my house coming up soon. The interesting thing about asking her that was there was no get together planned at all. I only asked because God said to and when she said yes, I now had a party to plan.

I called up my friends Sasha, Ari, Cassandra and a few others and told them we needed to plan a Chinese day. We invited some kids to learn about China and Taiwan. We also had some food and activities planned. The ladies in my sisterhood got right on it. Within a few weeks, it was all arranged. Cassandra organized a full Chinese buffet, Sasha and her daughters helped get things ready in the house. Others came ready to hear my new friend's testimony and to learn about her culture. The day finally arrived, and we were all there and ready. My new friend shared her testimony with us. It was so powerful. We were all crying. All the women there gathered around her afterwards and prayed with her and her children. I didn't realize it at the time, but that day she entered the sisterhood. Since then, that lovely lady from the library has been an integral part of my life. I am grateful to God for every sister He adds to my family. If you are a woman that doesn't have a sisterhood, start by connecting with a women's ministry near you. Join a Bible study, a life group, or community activity where you get to rub shoulders with some amazing people. If any man reading this does not have men they can call on, it's time for you to connect with godly men near you. It's important to have these relationships.

Seasons have come and gone for me. I have changed locations and experienced losses and gains of all kinds. But God is still adding to my sisterhood. Some of my newer friends may not realize it yet, but a few of them have already become so precious to me that I pray for them every day. I grew up having only one sister. However, God has filled my cup to overflowing with women that I call sisters. I know God speaks to me through their love. My family is large. I have many sisters. They come from all over the world and from almost every state in the USA. I have experienced greater hues of color, more meaningful adventures, and brilliance from the light of Truth in my life through these ladies, my sisterhood.

Lutefisk and Seders

"Let brotherly friendship continue; but don't
forget to be friendly to outsiders; for in so
doing, some people, without knowing it, have
entertained angels." (Hebrews 13:1-2, CJB)

"Love must be completely sincere. Hate what
is evil, hold on to what is good. Love one
another warmly as Christians and be eager
to show respect for one another. Work hard
and do not be lazy. Serve the Lord with a
heart full of devotion. Let your hope keep you
joyful, be patient in your troubles, and pray
at all times. Share your belongings with your
needy fellow Christians and open your homes
to strangers." (Romans 12:9-13, GNT)

My family loves spending time with people. Worshiping God, having great fun with others, and enjoying the great outdoors with friends and family is a joy. Our youngest son's favorite movie is about a family that moves from the city in the 70's and becomes a Wilderness Family. Both of my boys can gladly binge watch all three movies in that series, shouting at the TV the whole time, since the dad never carries a gun to protect them from the wild animals that always attack. As a family, we love hiking, hunting, fishing, growing food, and raising farm animals. We appreciate living places where we have enough space and privacy to have chickens, have a garden, and where the men in the house can "go to the bathroom" without going to the bathroom.

My husband Paul and I know that God can use anything for His glory, so we give Him everything to use. Paul and I love to share the love of Christ in diverse gatherings of people and cultures. Holy Spirit has opened many doors of friendship and ministry to us through hosting feasts and worshiping together in several Holy Spirit planned gatherings, like themed birthday parties, American holiday shin-digs, cultural celebrations where we explore and pray for different nations, Scandinavian Christmas dinners, and Biblical Feast celebrations. We love taking everyday occasions and turning them into a celebration of the goodness of God. We ask God throughout the year to show us how he wants us to display hospitality using the gifts He has given us, and he faithfully answers our requests and provides for the plans. Here is part of our journey of hearing from God in how we have been called to show hospitality.

Our first events as a young married couple were parties at our duplex for kids. The get-togethers were small, as you might expect in a tiny 500 sq. ft apartment, but they were exciting. We would watch Christian children's movies, eat cookies, and play outside. We found early on that keeping a selection of faith-based children's movies and music in the house was an excellent way to show hospitality to children in our neighborhood. Many of the children we were interacting with did not go to church and those tools were wonderful ways to connect in a way they understood. A little boy who lived across from us came and kept on coming. We started inviting him to church. His family were not Christians, but they saw that we were trustworthy people. We ended up taking him to church almost every weekend. Paul and I saved money so that little boy could go to church camp. There, he surrendered his life to Jesus. Over the next few weeks, we witnessed the change in this little boy. He was so proud to be a son of God. He saved up his own money and purchased himself a cross. Since he didn't have much money, it was an inexpensive one, but it was silver in color, at least three inches tall and on a silver chain. The precious child proudly wore that cross every day. Right before we moved from those apartments that little boy's grandmother came to visit him. She came over to thank us for spending time with her grandson. She said that she was a believer and had been praying for him for many years. This encouraged us to really trust God to use His gift of hospitality even more.

Over the next few years, Paul and I hosted both small and large gatherings. While we were doing our Master's in Teaching program at George Fox in 2003-2005, we were staying at a very "cost effective" apartment in Oregon. Once in that apartment, Paul was trying to put a water filter system on the pipes and the pipes were so rotted they crumbled right in his hands. The water was going everywhere. When we went to turn it off, the handle to do that crumbled. It was past midnight, so no help was coming until the morning.

It was in this apartment that we hosted an adoption party for my friend and her two new daughters. They stayed up late with us as we decorated and made a DVD of memories to show during the party. We had a long guest list. As people began to drive up looking for our place, I could see their concerned looks as I watched them from our third story window. I just smiled and ran to open the door. The guests came in and filled our place to the max. Paul and I catered that party with crackers, cut up cheese, and handed out lemonade. That's all we had the budget for. However, God really stretched that food and everyone there found joyful communion. I heard people saying how blessed they were to have come as they were leaving. I thanked God for helping us to be hospitable and asked Him to teach us how to grow in this gift.

We've always had a heart to see children develop and grow in the Word and the Spirit of God. While living in Washington, we would have parties for kids. We first began sharing the Feasts of Adonai (ex: Passover) with children before we ever extended it to adults. We would host child-centered Seders that were holistically focused on what drew kids into worship. On Easter, we would show Good Friday and Resurrection media to the children and do fun activities and discuss the sacrifice Yeshua made for us all. At other times, we would have scripture themed parties near birthdays. We would use the VBS curriculum and invite the children into worship and a relationship with Jesus. At Christmas, we pulled out every resource possible and used movies, toys, and skits.

One Christmas with the children was particularly special. A family nearby was caring for some children who had grown up in a very abusive Islamic home. We got to spend a lot of time with them. We simply asked if they wanted to hang out with us and the other kids. The children liked that idea and we played with nativity toys, we sang songs and danced, we talked about the tree of life, and we watched Christmas movies.

While watching a movie, one of the sons of this Islamic family yelled loudly. We were so startled in the room, we thought something had happened. He yelled again in his accent, "What! What! Is it true?! God came down to earth to become a man like me?!" I came near him smiling and said, "Yes, He did!" That young man stood there shocked and soaked up the rest of the movie till the end like a sponge. During the next few days, he visited us several times wanting to read all the children Bibles we owned. He watched a children's video series about the armor of God. In this series, a man who was changed by the word of God suits up with the armor of God to fight evil. That Islamic boy watched every episode at our house. He memorized all the verses about putting on the armor of God. Paul and I had never seen that level of zeal for the Word of God in a child before. It was beautiful. By the time Christmas came, he was all in with Jesus, and he wasn't turning back. That young man began to live like a person who genuinely believed in Jesus and he embraced the word of God like it was oxygen. He stated in conversations with us that Jesus was the sacrifice for his salvation, that he died, and rose again. This little boy acknowledged it with passion. He read everything he could in the children's Bible about the second coming of Christ and was very excited about this. He also expressed to us that he realized he was a sinner, though he didn't use that word, and he had clearly decided to believe that Jesus was the only way to God. His hunger for the Word was contagious. Before he left, we passed by a church that had a large cross at the top of it. This young man pointed to the cross and said, "I used to wonder what that was when I came here. Now I know. It means the power of God through Jesus." I pray for that young man often. He was the oldest son in his family.

When we moved to Maricopa, AZ, we had 1.25 acres, and a single family home large enough for hosting. It was a single level manufactured home. Never before did we have such space for gatherings. We filled our land with chickens, ducks, and turkeys. We loved raising them and it became a wonderful thing to have when we were hosting various parties with different themes. Once we hosted a superhero party for our kids' babysitter. That was so much fun. We all wore costumes and had to declare our superpower. My super strength was having eyes behind my head to see what my kids were doing when they didn't know it. Another time, we had a Native American themed party and invited some of my friends. We made crafts, listened to Native Christian music, and talked about prayer points. Then there was the Valentine's party where everyone made their own homemade pizza and we played a dancing exercise computer game.

One of the most creative social gatherings we've hosted is an outdoorsman party. Our boys love anything related to a well-known duck call outfit in Louisiana. Those gentlemen there have been amazing evangelists to my sons. Hence, we usually throw this kind of party near my oldest son's birthday. We go all out. Most of the guests would arrive in camo. All our best friends would pitch in and help. Cassandra, one of my best friends, and an amazing chef, would cook up all the delicacies from the cooking DVD associated with that duck call company our sons like, including frog legs and catfish, which happens to be two of my favorite foods in the world. They are always the first to go. There is always a full buffet at anything we host. I got that from my mom. We welcome the families to play games like shooting the fake ducks with rubber band guns. We go outside with our duck calls and blow them at our pet ducks and chickens. We would also share testimonies of what God has done in our lives. It was always a time of connecting and sharing God's love with each other. Everyone would leave blessed and encouraged.

Another way God gave us to show hospitality is with raising meat chickens and meat turkeys. We would buy a crazy amount, like 100, raise them from babies, and invite a few other families to join us in butchering them when they were ready to harvest. Every family was able to take an abundance of meat home with them. I absolutely loved the communion at these harvest celebrations. It's always full of merriment I loved the way all hands got busy. Some did the slaughtering, some worked the scalder, so the feathers would come out easier, while another group worked at the plucking table. We used to pluck our birds by hand, then we eventually purchased an electric chicken plucker. What a blessing that was. The most time-consuming job after we got the plucker was butchering the meat. With M.S., I don't do well with repetitive motion with my hands, but God has always blessed us with families who had excellent butchering skills. While our butchers do their job, the rest of us gut, clean, and seal the meat. The teamwork, the conversations, and the blessings are amazing. So much of the conversation at these harvest meetings easily leads to discussing the goodness of Jesus and the testimonies of the lives He's touched.

Sometimes I have dreams about details on how to host or plan a celebration. Sometimes when I dream or have visions, part of it is in Hebrew. I will have angels saying things to me in Hebrew, or I am shown signs or writing in Hebrew. In fact, it was a dream I had many years before we ever fathomed the thought of living in the Midwest, where God showed me in the dream at a typewriter writing THIS book in THIS house. In that dream, Jesus looked like a Native American man, He declared himself to be the chief of everything and He said we were in the Chief's Kindgom in the dream. He had Hebrew symbols on His arms. It wasn't until the Chief's won the super bowl, right where we live in Kansas City, that I fully understood how prophetic that dream was. In the dream, Jesus gave me a job to do, and it was to write. He told me to type Wind Song and to share our stories. He gave me this dream near Passover. Paul and I follow the different Feasts of Adonai (Passover, feast of booths,…), as well as Christmas, Easter, etc… We are enriched by the wealth of understanding it has given us of God and our roots as followers of Jesus. We aren't that traditional about it though. They often look very different from the official way of celebrating them.

One of my favorite hosting times is during the Christmas season. My husband's family has deep roots in Scandinavia and for many years did Christmas dinner the Scandinavian way. Every year sometime after St. Lucia day, Paul and I host a Scandinavian Christmas dinner. We do all the trimmings and we usually have lutefisk. We spare no expense with all the staple dishes of the Scandinavian Christmas season. Fish prepared in various surprising and old-world traditional ways, Pepparkakshus, Swedish roast chicken, Lucia buns, cardamom rolls, pickled herring, almond cake, Swedish meat balls, and my favorite, Jansson's temptation. We also plan some unique Scandinavian games, including the rapping game, where everyone takes turns making up a rhyme.

Paul and I use that time with our friends and family to share our family history and talk about some of the traditions. We discuss how Jesus changed the culture there and discuss current prayer points for Scandinavia. We also give praise to God for bringing his Word to the Scandinavians and for the move of God in the hearts of many there to follow Christ. The kids play games, build gingerbread houses out of pepparkakshus and roast marshmallows over the fire pit. Of course, since it is a Christmas party, we have an intimate worship time together. Sometimes, when we have the time, we have the children light candles and gather to lead us in Christmas worship songs. I love this because my husband's Scandinavian family came to America, in part, because of being persecuted for their faith in Christ. They were Baptists in a Lutheran country, and some even faced jail for it. I appreciate the history and love to share it and thank God for his goodness in our family with others. We host this feast as a gift for our children and our friends at Christmas to show them how much we appreciate them. We love celebrating Christ with them in this way, and this is my oldest son's favorite celebrational time of the year.

The Passover Seder and the Feast of Tabernacles are two of the biggest celebrations all year. We don't worry so much about accuracy of days and times on anything. We just pray about what day God wants us to host it and call up all our family and friends. They all pitch in and before we know it, my whole house is turned into a banquet hall with skits, songs, and interpretive dance performances. It's all very child-centered. In Arizona, our friend Cassandra, who also cooked for almost all our events, oversaw organizing the Kosher kitchen for these feasts. She's had many years of working in a kosher kitchen. Ari, another wonderful friend of ours, oversaw making sure decorations, seating, and many other aspects were planned out well. Ari is an extraordinarily gifted administrator. She is a blessing.

We had a host of many others who took jobs to make sure everything was in place and ready for the day. One of the young ladies always choreographed a messianic dance for the Seder every year. Also, God would always give an appointment to me through a dream on who was to sing the Shema, which would start our Seder. These feasts looked different every year in many ways and came with surprises each time. We would pray about how God wanted it to go every year and everyone participated in seeing the vision come to pass. The Passover Seder for many years was our largest feast, and it is my youngest son's favorite feast of the year. Then a few years ago, the Feast of Tabernacles began to grow. So much of what God has been doing lately in our lives and has spoken to us in recent years surrounds that time frame on God's calendar. We have an amazing time feasting, playing, singing in the night, playing our tambourines, and frolicking under the moonlight. There was always a sense of fullness, joy, and communion for all that came to any of our celebrations.

Our main goal with any celebration is that the name of Yeshua is made famous and that He is revealed as the living Truth. We ask Holy Spirit to teach us how to make our messages understandable to the children and adults. We try to foster an environment where people can connect and build relationships, where anyone can feel welcome regardless of their history. We go all the way with these celebrations and spare no expense of our time and effort. We have used every space in our home and every space outside. We have invited our guests to play with our animals, ride the golf cart, and occasionally you might catch a kid sliding down the solar panels, or hugging to death one of our turkeys due to their extreme form of affection. One year, we decided it was best to announce to parents to make sure their children understood the dangers of sliding down high voltage solar panels.

Almost all the families would bring a dish to share. In addition, many families would use their trucks to let us borrow their folding tables and chairs. Our church gave us sixty folding chairs. People would offer up their sound equipment. Doug, a faithful friend and musician, even led worship for us. It was always such a wonderful time. We always make clear that these feasts belonged to everyone, so all the families who came yearly pitched in gladly.

You may never be interested in hosting a feast like I described above, but we all are given chances by our Heavenly Father to extend ourselves in warmth and openness to those around us. Everyone can step into opportunities to partake in hospitality. It may look like working within a church or organization to see others blessed. It could be sharing from your own skills, time, and resources to create space for someone to experience the love of God. Whatever it is, it will be a sweet fragrance to our Creator. Hospitality is holy when God's love is being shared. I pray that you are encouraged to step out and spread your wings in the gift of hospitality. It is so good to break bread with one another, both believers in Jesus and non-believers. Hospitality creates bridges for God's love to flow to others. Hospitality is a gift that gives back to you when you give it. We have seen the hands of Jesus help us this past year through so many people, some of whom we have never met. I think of all the smiles in heaven when we worship God through hospitality.

> "Every day they devoted themselves to meeting
> together in the temple complex, and broke
> bread from house to house. They ate their food
> with a joyful and humble attitude, praising
> God and having favor with all the people. And
> every day the Lord added to them those who
> were being saved." (Acts 2:46-47, HCSB)

Opportunities

"He answered: Love the Lord your God with
all your heart, with all your soul, with all your
strength, and with all your mind; and your
neighbor as yourself." (Luke 10:27, HCSB)

"Instruct them to do what is good, to be
rich in good works, to be generous, willing
to share." (1 Timothy 6:18, HCSB).

We pass people every day. Some of us rarely notice the casual strangers we see in stores, parks, or even church. I have had to ask Jesus to forgive me many times for hastily moving through moments when Holy Spirit was clearly telling me to slow down and take notice. I am learning to pause in my daily activity more often and see those closest to me in the moment. I am learning how to notice the atmosphere near me and the people in it and to pray and act when God is asking me to. We are not alone in this world, and as I get older, I am developing a greater awareness of how prayer and kindness can create paths for God's love and goodness to flow in my world.

We all have our own sphere of influence. However, all believers in Jesus are called to be a light in the world for Christ. Because God made us all different, each of us has our own sets of gifts, abilities, and resources. Regardless of what we have, it is all given to us by our Lord. When we comprehend that He has created us to love as He loves, we are challenged to reflect on how we are doing this in our daily living. The more spaces of our lives we allow Jesus to live in, the more easily we can see the world through His eyes. This is not an easy thing when we have our own agendas, plans, and habits that don't always line up with what God has set before us. I ask the Lord every day to forgive me where I miss those opportunities and I thank Him for trusting me time and time again with new ones.

I can recall when my husband and I were newly married, Holy Spirit told me to give a friend of mine from college $50. Paul and I had very little money, maybe $80 to $90 ourselves. However, the conviction of this didn't go away. Paul and I talked about it and decided to give her $30. We thought we were doing good to do that much. A few months later, when we were having dinner with her and her husband at their apartment, she told us how they had been praying for God to help them pay a very important bill and they had been short $50. She said when we gave them the $30, they knew that even though it wasn't enough, God had heard their prayers. My heart just sank as she said those words. So did Paul's. It was painfully clear to us that because we gave of ourselves what we thought was best, rather than what Holy Spirit was calling us to do, we shortchanged a blessing for a dear friend. Right away, Paul and I put our money together and gave her the other $20. We told her that we know it's late and we missed the opportunity, but we had to give it to her. We told her we regretted missing that opportunity and we asked God to forgive us.

Sometimes the stakes are a little higher when we miss an opportunity to do good. I can remember when I was in my first year of kindergarten or maybe first grade, I missed a very important opportunity, but it was one I don't believe I knew how to act on. I was in a similar situation and felt trapped myself. I was walking out to the playground after lunch, which I did each school day. I had to pass the folded-up bleachers near the back door of the gym. That day, for some reason, I felt led to look behind the bleachers. When I did, I saw an older blonde-haired girl from one of the upper elementary classes behind the bleachers. She was with a little boy, whom I recognized from my kindergarten class. She was French kissing the little boy and she was touching him between his legs. When they noticed me looking at them, the girl became very angry. The boy seemed scared and looked like he had been crying. The girl told me to go away and that I better not tell anyone. The boy's eyes, which I shall never forget, were sending me a different message. Even though I felt conflicted about my own abuse that I was living in at the time, the tears that I saw in that little boy's eyes told me he wanted help. I went outside and sat the whole recess debating if I should tell a teacher. I should have. I didn't. As an adult, I pray for that boy every time I think of him. I know that I was in a bad place myself, but still I wish I would have done something.

Sometimes doing good takes more than casual effort. It may move you out of your comfort zone and require a greater amount of time and effort than normal. However, when Holy Spirit is prompting you to reach out to someone else, everyone is blessed, even you. Paul was given an unexpected opportunity to be the hands and feet of Christ while on a morning run in the deserts of Arizona. This is his story in his own words.

Paul's story

There is a mountain near our old house that was about a 5-mile round trip. At the top, there was a little cave that would sometimes contain what I thought were eagle eggs. It was a great way to get exercise. You could take a different path to the top, each with varying difficulty every time. At the top, you could see the whole of Hidden Valley, and there were Saguaro cacti everywhere.

I had fallen off the exercise bandwagon for about a month and I was really feeling like I needed to get back into it one morning at about 6 AM. It was still a little bit dark and already was feeling pretty warm outside. I started to jog down the road to where the road ended and the base of the mountain started. Along the way, there were a couple old manufactured homes sitting in the desert that looked abandoned. As I was passing one of them, I heard a faint yell. "Help me… Help me…" It sounded really muffled. It was so quiet that I thought it was my imagination. I stopped for about 30 seconds and stood in silence. I heard it again: "Help me". I realized this was not in my head! I started to wonder if it was a hostage situation or something. I was armed with my Glock 19, which was often the case after being robbed at gunpoint a year or two before, but that's another story. I yelled, "Does somebody need help?!" I didn't hear anything back, but I decided to head over to the old house in the desert a little ways off the road.

It turned out to be an old man that had fallen down. His shoulder was really hurting him. I helped him up, sat him on his old mattress, and then I sat on the floor while he called his brother up in Phoenix. It was going to be a couple hours before his brother could come down, so I was just sitting on the floor getting comfortable. I noticed that the room started to seem very peaceful and calm. He started to tell me about how he was going to get his life right with Jesus and was going to be a changed person from now on. Then, he told me all about when he was younger and his adventures in a honky-tonk band. He would tell me again about how he was going to get his life right with God from now on. I just listened. He had a lot of things to say. I don't think he got visitors very often. One thing that really struck me was that the peacefulness in the room was almost surreal. This was a divine appointment. His brother arrived after a while, and I lifted him up into the truck. He was a skinny old man, but was he heavy! I continued on my run and told Barbara about the whole thing when I got home.

Some time went by and Barbara made a Christmas card for him and put it in his mailbox (his gate was closed). A while later, we heard back from his niece. She proceeded to tell us how he had passed away the night I had stopped at his house to help him, but he was surrounded by his brother's family at the hospital. She said how his biggest fear had been to die alone. He kept telling them about "Paul", so they were curious to know who on earth that was. When they got the card, they were glad to make contact with us.

I started to see the peace I felt in that room as the presence of God. God knew how lonely he was, and it was his time to go Home, so I was brought along to be with him during that time.

******

I remember once when Paul and I were in Kenya at Christmas, I was very sick, and my family had gone out to town to get some fruit or something. We were on a very tight budget and had walked most of the way, but my body was shutting down and I wasn't doing well. Paul knew it and wasn't sure what to do as we didn't have the money to get a taxi. We just kept shuffling along slowly, taking breaks along the way. It was starting to get dark, and Paul was praying. Soon, a tuk tuk started coming up the street we were walking along. A tuk tuk is a like a rickshaw, except a motorcycle does the work instead of a bike or a person's two feet. They are common in many countries. The driver stopped near us and a lady (the passenger) in the tuk tuk told us to get in. She told the driver she was paying for our trip to wherever we were headed. This meant that she would get home later, as she had to wait until the tuk tuk driver took us home so that she could pay him for whatever distance it was. We were so grateful she was willing to sacrifice her time and money for us.

We were strangers to that lady in the tuk tuk, yet she obeyed the prompting of Holy Spirit and, in doing so, we were greatly blessed. She was literally answering a prayer we were just praying. I encourage you to follow what the Lord is leading you to do. If you know you have missed some of those opportunities like I have, just ask the Lord to forgive you. He forgave all of humanity on the cross for each and every one of our shortcomings. The opportunities to be the hands and feet of Yeshua aren't running out any time soon. God has plenty more to bring your way. Those opportunities may require your time, your money, or your prayers. Whatever you sense Holy Spirit leading you towards, accept it and give your best. You don't want to miss any opportunity to participate in a blessing that Holy Spirit has person-ally called you to be a part of. It is an honor to be invited by God to bless others, to take part in paving a path for His love and goodness to flow through.

What Thieves Do

"Therefore Jesus said again, 'Very truly I tell
you, I am the gate for the sheep. All who have
come before me are thieves and robbers, but
the sheep have not listened to them. I am the
gate; whoever enters through me will be saved.
They will come in and go out, and find pasture.
¹ The thief comes only to steal and kill and
destroy; I have come that they may have life,
and have it to the full.'" (John 10:7-10, NIV)

"I have told you these things, so that in
me you may have peace. In this world you
will have trouble. But take heart! I have
overcome the world." (John 16:33, NIV)

"The LORD appeared to us in the past,
saying: "I have loved you with an everlasting
love; I have drawn you with unfailing
kindness." (Jeremiah 31:3, NIV)

Satan is our real enemy. He's the one that schemes to steal, kill, and
destroy us. The enemy is constantly attacking our foundation in the
word of God. He wants us to walk in doubt. He doesn't have to even
take us to a place where we don't believe in God anymore. If he could
get us to a place where we believe God is not relevant to our lives, or
persuade our hearts to use phrases like, "I don't believe that a loving
God would" (fill in the blank), then Satan has succeeded in stealing
pieces of our God-given destiny. When we as humans make ourselves

the authority on defining "good" based on our own formula, we are declaring ourselves to be gods. The enemy has sometimes tricked us into believing that our own morality and definition of what's acceptable pain and suffering is more authoritative than God's. The enemy enjoys watching us, in our own self-deception, take a long journey away from Jesus. Satan's ultimate goal is not to make us axe murderers or evil villains. It's simply to detour us from Truth, which is Jesus who died for our sins and rose again. One of the most common ways that the enemy does this is through using our emotional responses to pain and trauma as proof against the ever-faithful truth of God's word. In these seasons of our lives, the enemy will attempt to sow seeds of doubt about God's sovereignty that lead us to question the authenticity of God being the very essence of love, peace, joy, goodness, and life. This is where many people begin to embrace lies from the greatest thief and liar of all, Satan.

Throughout history when nations are warned ahead of time that they are going to be attacked, robbed, or destroyed, they prepare themselves and their cities. They fortify their walls. They put on their armor and ready themselves for battle. This is exactly what believers should do, because we have already been warned. Jesus has already made it very clear that He is the only door and that the enemy of our soul is coming to steal that truth from us, kill our faith, and destroy our future. Satan loves to see us suffer. I don't just mean pain or trauma. I mean he loves to see truth suffer under the attack of our thoughts that come through our up and down emotional seasons of life. I'm talking about our faith in Jesus and our conviction that God is always good. The enemy seeks to keep us on shaky ground where we feel afraid of the difficulties that will surely lie ahead in our life's journey towards eternity. Satan has a full, well-practiced system of using our own frail emotional state when we are in crisis to feed us lies that sound more practical in our human evaluations. One thing I've learned through my years of living is to never trust your emotions in a time of crisis. Instead, hold on with every fiber of your being, to the truth of God's word. This is not to suggest our emotions are bad. Our emotions come from our Creator and we are made in His image. It's when our emotions have been ravaged by lies that we shouldn't trust them, when the thoughts associated with our emotions do not line up with what God says about us and about Himself. ALWAYS go by what the Bible says over what your heart is screaming inside. Your heart can lie to you depending on what you've allowed to grow there. If the soil your spirit was born into was thorny, rocky, or poor, then you must let Holy Spirit create new good soil for Truth to grow in. God's word is the most powerful weapon you will have against the lies the enemy brings your way. The best way to get fortified for a future battle is to prepare before trauma comes your way. Memorize scripture, write it down, post on your wall some key battle verses for the future fights that will wage in your head from time to time. Also, knowing a few key things that Satan wants to steal, kill, and destroy in our lives can help you prepare beforehand when pain and suffering comes.

Satan wants to destroy our ability to recognize godly love from others. When our ability to do that is damaged, it also greatly affects our ability to fully embrace how much we are loved by God. During my journey of sexual, physical, verbal, emotional, and spiritual abuse from my dad, I learned a lot about living in trauma. This is not necessarily a good thing, but I have experienced and seen firsthand how the enemy uses our pain and sufferings to rob us of our understanding of God's love for us and detour us from seeking intimacy with Christ. One of the greatest dysfunctions that happens to an abused person is that their antenna for detecting love that is healthy and that honors our Creator gets broken. When one of the people in a relationship is abusive and the other person doesn't recognize it, the person being abused becomes a victim. And, as a victim, they are constantly being mentally retrained by the abuser to believe that the abuser's behavior and actions are normal and healthy. In fact, what often happens is that the victim comes out of the relationship believing that there was something wrong with them, not the abuser.

I couldn't identify my own abuse for almost 14 years because everything and everyone in my environment affirmed my abuser as being normal and healthy. So, naturally, there had to be something wrong with me for feeling the way I felt. I was relying on my own emotional responses and thoughts as proof that the abuse I was receiving was normal. But what I didn't understand was that my emotional response and the thoughts that I believed were all birthed from lies that began through my father. It put me in an ugly cycle of believing things to be true about myself that were lies. Thus, people need to have others outside of themselves in seasons of pain and suffering to help them see with different eyes.

Even if a person is not in abuse, I find that people who have endured intense suffering and trauma sometimes believe that they deserve the outcomes of that suffering. This response keeps them in a place of suffering and breeds hopelessness, helplessness, and worst of all, a sense of feeling unloved. This is exactly what Satan wants. He wants everyone to have a broken antenna for detecting love so that we seek love outside of God and fill our need for love in ways that don't last, bring more pain, and fail to honor God. What Satan does is taint our minds and hearts with lies that convince us that we deserve what we are in, even if what we are in is evil, and that there is something wrong with us. To be clear, there IS something wrong with all of us. We are all sinners, and we all fall short of God's glory which is why we need Jesus. However, I am talking about the kind of self-blame that I had with my dad. He used to tell me that if I would only do this or that (sexually speaking), I would be a better daughter. For some people, it's if you did this or that you'd be a better spouse, or friend, or worker, or girlfriend. Perhaps you have a disability or an addiction and you have become convinced that if you could just get well or drop the addiction you would be a better, more lovable person. The truth has always been that God loves you no matter what state you're in! His love will never decrease for any reason. Furthermore, you can't do anything to cause Him to increase it because it is at full, maximum, everlasting love already! Of course, if you have an addiction, you need to get help to end it. As it is, Satan wants us to learn love from his broken perspective of it. The enemy wants us to carry that broken definition of love down through our generations. Don't let him rob you of intimacy with your Creator by convincing you that you are too broken or messed up to be loved.

Satan wants to kill your faith in God. Oftentimes in trauma, some people will question why a loving God would allow such things to happen. To start, I'd like to remind you that one of our gifts from our Creator is free will. At what point should God start taking that away from others? And who should He start with? In the end, every human on this planet would have a different plan for that idea. The other thing is this, we could ask why about a lot of things. "Why" is not a bad question at all. I love the why questions from those I teach. I love exploring the possibilities of the answers for those questions. Regardless of the varying answers, theories, and possibilities I may believe at any season of my life, none of them affects the reality that God loves me, God wants me, and breathed life into me so that I can be with Him. Although, when it comes to God, sometimes our "why" questions are being asked to declare our disagreement or defiance to something we grew up believing that may have had more to do with church culture, specific church doctrine, and national perspectives of faith in the country we grew up in. Sometimes, when different church doctrines or some Christians have perspectives we don't like or agree with, we get angry and pull away from Jesus. Sometimes, we insist on answers for some things but not for others. For example, why would a gust a wind blow and knock over my tea I just purchased while sitting outside the café? That's a simple question, however no one is going to have a fit over it. How about, why does the paper boy throw the paper atop my prized roses? Why would God allow the ear wax in my ear to fill up so much that I can't hear? Let's try, why did so many children starve today in India? Why did I have all those years of abuse? Why are so many unborn babies dying every day? Why can't I find a match for my socks!? I'll tell you why. Because we are sinners in a fallen world full of sin, chaos, and instability. That, and socks never stay together unless you use safety pins. We all have free will, and creation is groaning.

Life is full of trouble. That is a promise from Jesus. Yes, Jesus heals. That's a fact. I have been miraculously healed of certain things during my lifetime. But for other things I am "walking in faith" for my healing. Yes, God has moved mountains for my family. However, there are times when we have walked in faith over mountains knowing that God could have moved them if He had chosen to. Yeshua said we will have trouble, but we shouldn't fear because He has overcome the world. He also says that just as He suffered, we too shall see suffering. When trouble comes my way, I try not to take the "why me" approach. I say, "Why not me?" Of course, my first response is to pray for deliverance. I pray in faith and believe without doubt that God has a perfect plan. I ask His perfect will to be done in my situation. If He doesn't give me a door out of my circumstance, then I know He will give me every bit of courage to walk out whatever I'm facing. Jesus never leaves me, nor forsakes me. Thus, if I am going through something that God has graciously given me the strength to walk through, I simply thank God for trusting me with the journey. In Creation's story of humanity, I am just as qualified to walk out pain as the next person. In fact, when I am through that pain, I am going to be wiser, more prepared for my future, and have a story that showcases the power of Christ in my life that will be amazing because I'm always expecting miracles. There is a song I love from Jon Thurlow called "Strong Love." One of the verses of the song reminds me that I already know how my story ends. It ends with me and Jesus, together.

I have found that God always uses my pain, suffering, and traumas to grow and develop me. I had a dream in April of 2015 where Rabbi Yeshua was before me. Thousands of people as far as the eye could see were surrounding me. They all were singing in massive worship of Rabbi Yeshua. There were others who were dressed like Him in the dream throughout the group, but no one there called them Rabbi, and they too sang the worship to Christ. Only Jesus was called Rabbi. Rabbi Jesus, dressed in white, came to me to bless me. He held both my hands and said to me, "What was taken out of you was so that gold and sapphires will grow in their place." As soon as I felt His touch, his power surged through my body. He grabbed my hands three more times. Each time I felt the surge through my whole body and each time it was so strong I almost fell over. I woke up feeling the last surge. I have certainty that God uses all my pain, suffering, and trauma to bring forth His fruit in me. As Yeshua told me in the dream, He wants gold and sapphires to grow in me. I know that the troubles I face are refining me into the person God is growing me to be so that I can help and serve those I was created to serve.

The enemy wants to destroy your understanding of your value to God. Satan doesn't want you to stand strong during your seasons of pain and suffering. He will whisper to your heart that you are forsaken, forgotten, and that God is not there for you. All of that is a lie. If there is one thing I know with absolute certainty, it's that God is always there. The best way to fortify your mind and heart in trauma is to recite or memorize the truth from the Bible that deals with the lies you are hearing. Say them day and night, don't let them leave your heart. Put them on the doors of your home, your walls, your fridge. You want to constantly remind yourself of the fact that you are not forsaken.

Another important thing is getting into a community of believers who can encourage you and support you on the days when doubt and pain is high. We all have days like that. None of us are super Christians. If you are disabled and can't get out to a community, watch Christian television and listen to Christian radio. There are wonderful channels and stations that offer 24 hours a day seven days a week programming where you can stay connected to God's Truth; and they have prayer lines and people to talk to. God has a community for you, but you must look for it. I have core people that I go to in my times of sadness and depression who remind me that God is with me and helping me all the time. The third thing I would suggest is that you start making a memorial in a notebook to remember what God has done and has promised you. You can write down all the things God has done for you and the amazing miracles you've seen, not just in your own life, but in the lives of those around you. Read that list of things often so that whenever the enemy is bombarding your mind with lies that God is powerless in your circumstance, you will be fortified by the reality of what God has done. The key to dealing with many issues related to pain and trauma is not just to keep the word of God flowing in your life, but you also must be vigilant to pull the weeds out of your soul garden and keep Satan from planting new seeds of lies in your mind and heart.

Satan seeks to kill your confidence in God wanting to use you. He wants you to assume all pain and suffering is a tool to punish or harm you. He wants you to believe the lie that you've been handed whatever pain you have as proof of your lack of usefulness for the Kingdom. Sometimes if you feel useless too long, it affects your ability to even connect with God. His goal is to use pain and suffering to confuse you into believing it's a punishment or a curse and that it isn't possible for God to move through you while you are suffering. The enemy wants to use your suffering and pain as leverage for his demonic plans to steal you away from understanding just how loved by God you really are and how worthy you are through the saving blood of Yeshua to be used by God. God wants to use everything to grow you and encourage others around you through beauty that can develop in you through your seasons of brokenness. In addition, God is certainly not interested in any measurement of what we think our usefulness or worthiness is. God doesn't love us for what we do. He just loves us. One of the most precious times in my journey of pain with my diagnosis of M.S. was getting occasional cards in the mail or notes telling me how encouraged the sender was by watching how I navigated my journey with joy and peace, trusting my God.

Some people want pain and suffering to all go away. Everyone can experience relief from the spiritual oppression of pain and suffering on earth because of the healing power of God in their lives. Likewise, everyone has the opportunity to know the healing power of God once they encounter Jesus. Many people around the world have already had miraculous physical healing through the power of Christ. All pain and suffering will go away ultimately for all believers in Yeshua. However, while we are here on our broken planet with our less than perfect lives, one of our jobs is to walk in faith. We are called to rise above our circumstances and allow the miracle of God in us to shine to those around us. After all, one of the greatest miracles is that God chooses us as His temple! Let's take physical challenges as an example. The fact that there are disabled people, and those who have experienced great suffering, has made the world richer. It encourages us to move in compassion in ways that we would not have acted before. Those that suffer give others the opportunity to love as Christ tells us to and remind us that God uses everyone, broken bodies, broken hearts, the mentally ill, and those with broken spirits. God wants us all! He doesn't want to leave any sheep that hear his voice behind.

I encourage you that the next time you feel too broken to be wanted or used by God, tell the devil he's a liar. You know, he really is a liar and I think it is important for us to keep that in mind when we are living out pain. Satan likes to take a tiny bit of truth and mix it up with a bunch of demonic mumbo jumbo that can sound sort of valid to the wounded or jaded soul. You should keep in mind that he is the father of all lies. It says so right here in John 8:44; read it and check it out. When you embrace this truth, you can navigate your feelings away from doubt and closer to what God says. There is no amount of suffering you could ever reach that would make you unworthy to be used for the kingdom of God. Just you being you, in whatever emotional, physical, or mental state you are working through can be a testimony to many people when we surrender our lives to Jesus. We don't have to do anything but embrace the love God is lavishing on us. I promise you, if you live loved, you will shine bright.

Satan wants to steal your identity. He wants you to believe that who you are is what your pain or suffering has offered you. He wants you to define your identity by your experiences, the wounds of your pain, your losses, and your own self-determined morality. The way to deal with this is to have a clear understanding from the word of God who you belong to and embrace that God didn't make a mistake when He created you. Our identity should always be defined by God and his Word, not by outside things such as abuse, loss of employment, divorce, a bad breakup, the death of someone we love, or our responsibility to our spouse or children. When we understand our identity in reference to our Creator, when life shakes us up and the world tries to redefine us based on current trends and ideas, we can stand on who we know we were created to be according to the word of God.

All of this is great information. However, when you are going through a traumatic experience like abuse, divorce, the loss of a child, you almost can't help but feel a little less than, a little broken, a little messed up. Therefore, we need to rely on the Word, which is our standard of truth, to define who we are in any circumstance. A good example from my own life is that I could easily have turned to women for affection, or I could have given myself over to multiple men using my broken antenna. I surely had a broken antenna for identifying godly, healthy love for a very long time. However, it was the word of God and the constant renewing of my mind that allowed me stay connected to who I was created to be. Because of this, the enemy was not able to steal my identity. Whatever has happened that may cause you to question who you really are and what your desires really should be, seek your answers from God in His word. Holy Spirit will lead you through the scriptures and help your heart to begin to understand your identity. Also, the more intimate you become with Christ, the more your desires will be to follow God's heavenly plan for your life.

Satan wants to destroy your future in eternity with Christ. He's a thief. And he often uses the same old bag of tricks. He might package it differently, but the root of it is the same old lies. The enemy wants you to have such a fractured perspective of God, His love for you, and His faithfulness to you, that you slowly drift away from Christ. He wants to destroy the wealth of treasures that God has prepared for you before you were born. Satan wants you to defy Gods plan for your life and deny yourself the blessings of living in God's grace. This is his ultimate plan for your future, to turn you away from trusting in Jesus. He knows following Jesus is about surrendering every part of your life to God's will and living the life God has for you. Don't give up in your journey of following Yeshua. When you sin or you find yourself struggling through pain, addictions, and difficult life traumas, surround yourself with believers who will help carry you to the truth.

No one is perfect. I look forward to joining an international, eternal adoration party, with formerly broken people like me, where there is never ending love, peace, joy, goodness, and life. That's who Jesus is! In His presence, all these things are birthed and given. When you find yourself in the fires of life and you think your boat is sinking, look to our savior Yeshua. He is always there! Don't let the shame from your past make its way into your present. God invented recycling you know; He will use everything in your life for His Glory. In your hurt, He is inviting you to Trust that He is the author of good, the identity of love, and the distributor of peace. When you are going through it, and we all do, don't let the enemy steal the seeds of your faith in God. Furthermore, guard the garden of your soul against the enemy's attempts to plant his own dysfunctional seeds. Ask Holy Spirit to awaken you to the presence of the living Christ in your circumstance, and never stop expecting miracles.

Walking Through the Storm

"While they were sailing, Jesus slept. A big
storm blew across the lake, and the boat began
to fill with water. They were in danger. The
followers went to Jesus and woke him. They
said, 'Master! Master! We will drown!' Jesus
got up. He gave a command to the wind and
the waves. The wind stopped, and the lake
became calm. He said to his followers, 'Where
is your faith?' They were afraid and amazed.
They said to each other, 'What kind of man is
this? He commands the wind and the water,
and they obey him.'" (Luke 8:23-25, ERV)

"For whatever was written in the past
was written for our instruction, so that
we may have hope through endurance
and through the encouragement from the
Scriptures." (Romans 15:4, HCSB)

When God is calling us into a new location, church, or season, He almost always lets us know ahead of time, as well as what to expect in the transitions. Of course, sometimes He surprises us. However, there are always signs before major transition. We had been going to a great church in Maricopa. As I said previously, we had been directed there by God when we moved to Arizona. We were involved in many things, including teaching Sunday school and participating in Bible studies. We had a full community there. Some of our core friends today have come from that church. The church was growing

185

and making plans to get a bigger place. I even had dreams about the future of that church. However, one thing we've learned through the years is that just because things are going smoothly doesn't mean that you will stay in the situation. God had other plans in mind for my family. One day, God gave us our transfer papers.

It was March 8, 2015, and I dreamed that Paul, the kids, and I were in a place where we were worshipping that was near where we lived. An angel came and told us, "Pack up your ministry and take it to a building on the other side." The messenger showed us the place by directing us visually toward it. In the dream, I had hawk-like vision and could zoom out and I saw that the building was far on the other side beyond the vast desert. In addition, a great wall separated where we were and where that place was. It was late in the afternoon in the dream and the building on the other side was in a mini-mall sort of place. I could see every detail of the building, but no name was shown to me as to where it was or what it was called. In the dream, Paul got very excited and started to pack up our ministry in boxes so that we could start transferring it to the new place. It was dark on our side of the wall, but I noticed with my hawk-like eyes that it was daytime where the building was. My eyes had to travel far down a long desert road before I could see any details of it. I saw that people at the building were trying to fix up something. They had paint and other things for lighting, and they were working on something.

I felt concerned in the dream, and Mrs. Hills my, principal from my childhood Christian school, (it was really an angel using her face) appeared. She said that Holy Spirit will teach us. Suddenly, I was assigned to transport some of the boxes Paul packed to the building. I began to walk into the dark night of our side towards the great wall. An opening was created in the great wall and I could see the other side and the light ahead. As I continued walking, a dramatic storm rolled in. It was so powerful it overturned big trees and shook the fixtures off the great wall. I was very afraid and it felt like I was going to die. I was afraid of the storm and I was too scared to go through the opening of the great wall. My friend Sasha appeared on my left side and said, "This opening was created by God. This is the time to walk through it." Then I knew it was going to be okay. Sasha disappeared and I started to walk through the storm towards the opening in the great wall. After that I woke up. I wrote this dream down and told no one, not even Paul.

I didn't tell Paul because, whenever I am shown things about a major life transition of any sort, I wait for God to reveal it to Paul as well. When Paul tells me the same thing, I know it's time to let him in on what I've been shown. That way, we have clear confirmation on all major transitions of our lives. It was the same way with writing this book. I got a word, and the Lord told me that He gave Paul the details. So, later that day I asked Paul what Holy Spirit had spoken to him that day. His answer had all the details just like the Lord told me. Paul confirmed everything I needed confirmed and I knew God clearly wanted us to write this book. After having the dream about going to another church, I waited for Paul to get confirmation. I had another dream a few nights later about being in the same church. This time the leaders in the church all had hammers and paint brushes in their hands and they were talking about how they had to get ready for the move. They talked about a cross in their new building, fixing up an office and they asked me in the dream if I could help them paint.

As it turns out, on March 14, 2015, Paul confirmed what I had dreamed on March 8th. He told me that he felt in his spirit that our season was done where we were worshiping in Maricopa and that God had another place for us, but that he didn't know where. I told him that God showed me where it was visually, and I shared all the details of what I saw with Paul. However, God didn't give me an address or name of the church. I did tell Paul that it was very clear in the dream that the church was far away.

Thinking about all the storm issues in the dream and how frightened I became in the dream, I decided I would share with my friend Sasha about us going to another church. She and I stood in my kitchen at the island and chatted. I told her that Paul believed our season was up where we were and that God had another place for us to go. I wanted to tell her about the dream also, but before I could say anything more, she said to me, "This is an opportunity created by God for you guys to serve Him. Walk through this door

He's created." Instantly, I realized that the real Sasha said almost the exact same thing that the dream Sasha said. Not only that, but the real Sasha was also standing on my left side and in the same way, just like in the dream. God used her to confirm this transition.

We called our church Sunday school director and told her the whole story. She was excited for us and asked if we could teach for a few more weeks. We said that we would keep teaching Sunday school for a month while they worked out the schedule. However, we spent the later hours of church on Sundays trying to visit new places. We cheated at first and visited the churches on the outskirts of our town, but none of them were where we were called. We knew in our hearts that the church was much farther away, but we got a chance to visit some very nice churches that month. Finally, after our Sunday school teaching was done, we woke up on a Sunday morning and just looked up churches in other cities that were not close to us. One of the church names that popped up was Two Rivers Church. The web-site for this church was in transition, so there was no picture of its outside. However, we thought the name Two Rivers Church sounded interesting. Since we had no clue how to find the building in my dream, we decided to go and visit Two Rivers Church just because the name sounded cool. On the way there, we drove in directions we had never driven before. It was in a city we had never driven to. Halfway there Paul said, "This will be the only time we go here; this is way too far." Then finally, we got to the main road. As we began to turn into the shopping center parking lot the church was in, Paul slowed down, almost to a total stop and said, "This is exactly as you described to me." It was very interesting to see this building in real life. We went inside, and the pastor was talking about the new build-ing they were moving to in a couple weeks. He was asking if anyone wanted to help paint and talked about the cross and office that they fixed up at the new building. We knew that was our new church home and had planned to come back the next week. Unfortunately, we didn't make the next Sunday. A great storm came.

My Uncle, who was very dear to me, passed away that week. We made plans to drive down with the kids to Texas for the funeral. All of our family was going to be there, and we were looking forward to seeing everyone. Also, that week, I started having some major M.S. symptoms. I was not doing well. We loaded the kids in our car, took all their favorite things and electronics, and my husband's work computer with his engineering schematics and programming on it (two years of work not backed up anywhere). We took special things for our family and started on our journey to Texas. The car started having engine trouble on the way down, but after a very long drive we finally arrived at my aunt's house. We met some family there and had a wonderful time, but that wasn't where we were staying for the evening.

At around 1 AM, we drove to my cousin's apartment to stay with him. We got there safely and got a few things out the car before parking on the street. I noticed we forgot my husband's work computer in the car and suggested he go get it. Paul went out to get the computer. I was upstairs in my cousin's apartment chatting when suddenly I got a vision of my husband laying on the ground in the night with blood pouring from his mid chest through the NASA shirt he was wearing. I instantly started to pray. I knew that something was going wrong outside. I prayed and asked angels to protect him and the blood of Yeshua to cover him. We waited in the apartment long enough that even my cousin began to wonder what was taking Paul so long to return. Then finally, the front door flew open, and there was Paul, bent over about to pass out. His face looked pale. He was terrified. He couldn't even speak at first. He had to calm down to tell us that he had been held up at gunpoint and that our car keys were stolen, his computer, and the car and everything in it was taken. This is Paul's experience in his own words.

Paul's Story

I was walking to the car at like 1:30 in the morning. I had to squeeze through a big, metal gate that could only be opened by people entering the apartment when they entered a special password on a keypad. I opened the trunk of our car, took out my laptop, and also grabbed a pull-up diaper. I thought John might have an accident and, when you are sleeping in someone else's bed, that's never good! It seemed like a nice night. I was meandering back to the metal gate, and a guy was running up behind me. I stood there so I could see what he wanted to say. When he ran up, he said, "Give me all your money, your wallet, your keys, cell phone…" I noticed that he had a handgun held really low near his right hip. It looked like a .357 revolver. This whole situation was not registering with me at all. I was just standing there, and was like, "Um… What? Okay. Here's my computer. Here's my wallet and keys." I gave him the diaper too, but that ended up on the ground. I guess he was potty trained at this point and saw no need for that.

Then, he just stood there, pointing the gun at me, with his other arm full of my laptop and keys. He wasn't saying anything. He just stood there for what felt like an eternity. I started thinking that he believes I'm a liability and could identify him. So, after a long delay, I said, "I have a wife and kids." Then, it seemed to snap him out of what his plans were. He said, "I don't care about your wife and kids." Then, He started to run away, turning around one last time to call me a female dog. I just stood there for a second, then walked slowly back, and that turned into a run back to the apartment. It's a weird feeling to have your life in the hands of someone who doesn't have any value for human life. It really was just by the grace of God that our kids were not fatherless, and my wife not a widow after that day."

******

The next day, my cousin drove Paul, our boys, and me to the pre-funeral activities, since we no longer owned a car. It was an interesting week. So much was going on, but God was so gracious to us. My family all pitched in and raised funds for us. People gave us clothes and shoes to wear. We were stuck in Texas for a little while after the funeral. However, God had a plan for that as well. My sister-in-law called us and told Paul that an old high school friend of theirs was now a commercial airline pilot and said he could help us get plane tickets back home. We called up that friend and he got plane tickets for like $30 each. Paul had no I.D., since his wallet was stolen, so our friend Sasha, who was taking care of our chickens, checking our mail, and watching our house, found copies of legal papers for Paul and sent pictures of them to us.

When we got back to Arizona, Sasha picked us up. Another friend from our homeschool co-op had an extra car and loaned it to us. So many people pitched in to help us. When we arrived back at our new church, we had truly walked through a terrible storm.

Most people would like for their lives to stay calm and stable. However, sometimes storms do come. When they come, we can't always avoid them, go around them, or have shelter from them. Sometimes, you've just gotta walk through it. This was one of those kind of storms for us. I always view storms as chances to demonstrate what we've learned from the word of God. They are also opportunities to exercise our faith. I don't think you can grow without trials. I am grateful that our extended family and the body of Christ was there to support us. They love us very much. I was very blessed to have the support of my cousin, who we stayed with during this crisis. I believe that experience has bonded him to my family in a special way. I am most grateful that God did not allow my husband to get killed. I am so grateful about that. God is always so gracious to me. I am blessed to say we walked through that storm and made it to the other side alive, together. Thank your Lord for your goodness. It follows me always.

> "Lord! I'm bursting with joy over what you've
> done for me! My lips are full of perpetual
> praise. I'm boasting of you and all your works,
> so let all who are discouraged take heart. Join
> me, everyone! Let's praise the Lord together.
> Let's make him famous! Let's make his name
> glorious to all. Drink deeply of the pleasures
> of this God. Experience for yourself the
> joyous mercies he gives to all who turn to hide
> themselves in him." (Psalm 34:1-8, TPT)

191

He Calls Me Bethany

> "One of the elders said to me, 'Don't cry. Look,
> the Lion of the tribe of Y'hudah, the Root of
> David, has won the right to open the scroll
> and its seven seals.'" (Revelation 5:5, CJB)

From the moment most people are recognized in the womb, they are given names. These names hold meaning that sometimes calls out purpose and potential in the person carrying the name. You see this in the Bible often. Countless hours are spent by dads and moms around the world thinking about what to call their baby. Some people are born under unique naming customs, while others are born into more stressful life circumstances. My friend, Ann, who lives in Africa, had one of these situations. She was orphaned, never adopted, and so she named herself. As an adult, a supportive Christian family gave her their last name. But all of us, no matter who we are or what circumstances we were born into, need a name that calls us forth into the vision for who and what we were created for. We need a calling from God.

God has a plan for a blessed life for each of us. He has named us all. Through His Spirit we have the power to live our life based on who He has declared us to be, not our circumstances, family story, or traumas. Jesus says in John 10:14 that He is the Good Shepherd. He goes on to say that He knows His sheep. The Word of God doesn't lie. It is the truth that all truth must flow from and the foundation by which all thoughts should be measured. Jesus (Yeshua), being the living word, declaring that He knows His sheep, tells me that anyone who seeks to know who they really are should seek Him.

I was given a birth name. It means "beautiful stranger," but through my relationship with Christ, I am learning daily who I really am in His eyes. I've shared many stories of how I overcame my struggles in my life and how I began to understand my identity as God's daughter. Of all my time with Jesus, there is a very significant experience I had as an adult. It is one of my most precious moments.

On May 24, 2015, Jesus came to me in a vision. I was lying in a guest bed in my son's toy room in terrible pain all over my body, unable to stand or move very well. This happens sometimes, I think a symptom of M.S. I was lying there, praying and meditating on my healing verses, as is my custom to do in situations like that. When Jesus first visually emerged, He came as a large African woman with long thick, braids and big strong legs. God wore a floral dress and had a comb. I knew it was Jesus (Yeshua), because ever since I was little, many times when Jesus comes to sit with me, He comes with flowers either on Him, with Him, or near Him, regardless of how He chooses to look in that instance. In this vision, God told me that I had to see something.

He came to my bed. As He touched me, I sat up in the bed. He sat on the bed and positioned Himself, causing me to lean against the big strong legs He had. As I leaned against them, I could feel the strength in them. He began to comb my hair. This was a beautiful experience for me. As a child, some of my favorite times with my mom were when she would comb my hair, so this really touched me in a deep way. The Lord was talking to me while He combed my hair. As God began to speak to me, He didn't call me by my name. He called me Bethany. This puzzled me at first, because that's not my birth name. When I looked back, He was not an African woman with braids anymore, He was a vast, translucent light of great magnitude. I knew it was still Jesus. He called me Bethany again. Then I understood that this was not just a name He was giving me, but was speaking to me of how He saw me. I had an internal understanding of not only love in Him calling me Bethany, but a sense of my calling and purpose wrapped up in it. Jesus wanted to show me something. He told me to look at the wall on the other side of the room I was resting in. I was so caught up in the vision, looking at the wall reminded me of the fact that I was still resting on the futon in the kids' toy room. Sometimes in these beautiful moments with the Lord I can almost forget where I am. On the wall appeared what He wanted to show me. It was an amazing sight to see! While this was progressing, Jesus turned into a lion and began to sing to me. Ahhhh! I wish you could have been there. Jesus (Yeshua), the Lion, sang a beautiful indescribable song to me, over me, and through me all at the same time. I laid back down in the bed and closed my eyes until I just went into a peaceful sleep. What a wonderful way to rest! Eventually, I woke up again. I told my husband Paul about it when he came into the room a few hours later to see if I felt okay enough to go to church.

It was a bright and sunny Arizona Sunday morning, and almost time for church to start. My body had a renewed strength which allowed me to be able to get out of bed and get dressed, though I still could barely walk. Despite the business of getting the kids ready and nearly an hour drive there, we made it to church on time. After the service, during prayer, Paul walked me to the front to be prayed for. I still wasn't feeling well and my heart was palpitating. This was only our second time at Two Rivers Church, so we didn't know anyone yet. At that time, almost everyone at the church was a stranger to us. No one knew about my health situation. A young lady prayed prophetically over us, not knowing my diagnosis or the visitation from the Lord I just had that day. In her prayer, she asked God to heal my heart. She also said to me that there will be a resurrection in my life, that I will sing and that my current afflictions were present for that place in time to show God's work in me. She went on to prophetically tell my husband and me that our whole household would see the fullness of God in our lives.

She prayed for my husband, one of our sons, and for other things as well. But the one thing that stood out to me the most was what she said at the start before she started praying. She said to me, "There is a song being sung over you as you are walking up here. I know that Heaven is singing over you right now." I didn't comprehend everything I was being shown in that vision, nor what it all meant for the future, but I know Jesus will be with me through everything. I know He will reveal and grant me the understanding we will need to navigate what He has planned. He is my greatest love. I can lean on His strength. He combs my hair, bringing wisdom and life to me. I am letting Christ define me. He has called me by name.

You don't have to have an experience like I had to know that Jesus has named you. God doesn't have the "one-size fits all" for how He shows His love. God goes through great lengths to reach all of us in very different and beautiful ways. Become intimate to what it looks like and sounds like when Jesus is trying to get your attention. The word of God puts it this way: He stands at the door and knocks. What does that knock look and sound like in your life? Jesus wants to sit with us in the living room of our hurt. He considers it worth dying for to clean out that dark basement in our soul. He's a perfect organizer of all that junk we keep in our secret closets. He's the only good exterminator for that pesky rodent, despair. He seeks to be present with us in our waiting, and in our brokenness. He is our healer. Jesus is always sending reminders to us of how to overcome. Jesus doesn't just knock at the door when things are tough. He wants to sit with us in joys, achievements, and in our calm, quiet times.

The verdict is out, Jesus died for you! On top of that, He rose from the dead and lives! He is the only one who has won the right to open the scroll. If He, the scroll opener, saw you so valuable that He died for you, then you really need to realize that He longs to commune with you. You are His greatest treasure. I invite you to step out of the theory of His love and into the reality of it. Learn what Jesus is calling you to. You can only find out by getting closer to Him. Intimacy with Jesus brings us closer to seeing His heart. Yes, people still call me by the name my momma gave me. That is the name by which the world knows me. I like it. However, whenever Jesus calls me, I always know it's Him. He calls me by a different name. What God calls me to is what I want to embrace above all else. He calls me Bethany.

"From a distance Adonai appeared to me,
saying, 'I love you with an everlasting love; this
is why in my grace I draw you to me. Once
again, I will build you; you will be rebuilt,
virgin of Isra'el. Once again, equipped with your

tambourines, you will go out and dance with the merrymakers.'" (Jeremiah 31:2-3, CJB)

About Bethany:

Bethany was a village on the Mount of Olives. The olive tree represents God's Temple, the Holy of Holies and the renewal of the kingdom of God. Zechariah 14 prophesies about the day of the Lord when His feet shall stand upon the Mount of Olives. Matthew 24 records when Jesus sat on the Mount of Olives and told his disciples what signs to expect for His return and the end of the age. Bethany was where Lazarus, Martha, and Mary lived, and where Lazarus was raised from the dead. Jesus made Bethany His home base for His ministry in his final days. Jesus also stayed the night on the Mount of Olives at Gethsemane before His arrest. The Gospel of Luke describes the Lord's appearance to his disciples after He rose from the dead. In the account, Jesus talks to them and guides them towards Bethany. In Luke 24:50, Jesus was taken up into heaven in the vicinity of Bethany. Bethany, an Aramaic or Hebrew word, means "house of affliction" and "house of song." In addition, Bethany is known as the "house of dates." Dates symbolize victory, faith, and abundance. In the Bible, a person with a zeal for doing good and for serving others from the heart of God's love is like a date palm. Bethany can also be referred to as the "house of figs." In the Garden of Eden, fig leaves covered Adam and Eve. Figs are a symbol of doing good to honor God also. It is also a symbol of wellness and having a safe place. The shade of one's fig tree speaks of peace and security. Figs take time to grow, develop, and mature. A healthy and vibrant fig plant is one where the gardener has been faithful to tend to it carefully over many years. In addition, the fig represents Israel in scripture. Bethany also means "house of poor." "How blessed are the poor in spirit! For the Kingdom of Heaven is theirs." (Matthew 5:3, CJB). The place where Bethany was located during the time the disciples and Jesus walked the earth is now known by the name of el-Azariyeh or Lazariyeh, "place of Lazarus," and it is located on the West Bank.

The Building God Built

"For every beast of the forest is Mine,
The cattle on a thousand hills.
I know every bird of the mountains,
And everything that moves in the field is Mine.
If I were hungry I would not tell you,
For the world is Mine, and all it
contains." (Psalm 50:10-12, NASB)

Sometimes God gives us unexpected surprises. Paul and I often get them around certain feast and holiday times of the year. It was in the spring of 2018 that we got one of the biggest gifts, size wise, that God has ever given us. This gift was seed that literally moved us into the future that God had in store for my family the coming year. It was through the obedience of several people, faithful friends, some associates, and one stranger that we would witness one of the most creative financial miracles of our time living in Arizona. This is the story of the building that God built and how He used it for His glory.

My friend Sasha, a good friend and prayer partner, called us one day and said that she had seen a vision of a large building on our property. She said she saw us putting lots of things into it. Sasha has pretty good accuracy on when God shows her something, so I tucked that one away to pray about. And it got me to thinking about buildings that we could build. About a month or so later, we got a phone call from my friend Ari, who oversaw organizing all the major logistics of the Seder. She would not have considered herself a person that goes around giving prophetic messages to people by any means. However, she had been given one by God to give us. I could hear it in her voice over the phone, the absolute certainty in her spirit about what she was given to tell us. Ari said that God told her that He was going to build a building on our property and that it would be there before Passover. I got excited and began thinking about what Sasha had told me not too long before. I told Ari that we didn't have any money and perhaps we should pray about how to raise funds. Ari quickly responded with authority in her voice, "No! It was very clear to me that you are not to pay a penny for this building." I thought to myself, "How exciting!" I got off the phone full of anticipation. I had already begun thinking about buildings and what I might want in one. I wanted a large garage door, a least one regular door, insulated, capable of being air-conditioned if needed, and I wanted it to be large. I went online and began to imagine the possibilities of what might come.

Over the next 10 days or so, I had two companies call and offer me buildings that others had paid for, but because they didn't want to drive them all the way back to Canada, they wanted to drop them on our property if we gave them $2000. I remembered what Ari said, "You won't pay even a penny for the building." So, I passed those opportunities up. Then, some business associates drove up and felt led to help us fix up our current smaller shop on our property. I was thinking to myself, God is giving me little breadcrumbs on what he's about to do. It was exciting to see the power of God moving in this season of waiting.

About a week or so after that, my husband, whom I had not talked to yet about my conversations with Sasha and Ari, got an interesting email from someone who followed his work with motor controllers. The man wrote, "Hi Paul, I see you always doing work with electric motors out of your bedroom or that crappy shop you guys put together. How about I build you guys a building?" Paul said no. A few days passed. He said, "Oh, just a little one. Maybe 1000 square feet, 15 foot at the middle." Paul was thinking, since when is a 1000 square foot shop little? Our other shop was 196 square feet so that we wouldn't have to get a building permit. Paul once again said, "No." About a week went by. Another email! Paul said no. This went on about 7 times. Finally, the guy said, "Look. I don't tithe. All those stupid churches are just out to steal everybody's money. I made a bunch of money from Bitcoin last year. Just let me do something nice for you! There are no strings attached!" Then on Sunday, as we are going to church, Paul casually tells me about the guy and what he was proposing to do. I felt a little bad that I hadn't mentioned to Paul before about what I knew God was doing. I told him everything. He said that he already had said no several times. We figured, if the stranger was the person to carry out God's prophetic word, then he'd contact us again. And he did. This time, Paul told him he could build a building for him, but keep it small.

Of course, the gentleman was hearing from God very clearly and did exactly what God told him to do over what Paul had suggested. In a short amount of time, we were emailed the plans for a purchased building that had a garage door, a regular size door, insulation included, additional plans for adding an air conditioner, and all other trimmings for being storm proof. I love it when people hear the Holy Spirit and obey. We are so very grateful and blessed by the obedience of the man who purchased the building for us, but I love how God has a sense of humor as well. I assumed that the building would be built by Passover. It did arrive a few days before Passover week, in pieces. I got a kick out of that and was so blessed to see a such a miracle just sitting on our property. I would walk by each piece and each box and thank God for it. Many of the people who regularly came to the Seder were deeply moved when they saw the fulfilment of what God had done. Some of us walked around the pieces and prayed. We all began to pray for help getting the building put together.

The building needed a concreate slab for its foundation, and I mean a big one! It was required to be about a foot thick and was going to cost around $12,000. We also could not afford to pay anyone to put the building together. We searched over the next few weeks and month and was unable to find any help within the range of our limited budget. God wasn't done yet. When God sets a plan in motion, He provides for it to completion. Around this time, we got a package in the mail. We didn't open it right away. The guy who bought the building asked Paul if he had the cement slab taken care of yet. "No. We are going to be saving toward that."

"Did you get that package I sent to you?"

"Oh yes, I saw that. Was that the charger connector you had told me about before?" (He had told Paul he was going to send him a little charger plug for something Paul was working on).

"Well, ya, but you really should open that box."

"OK."

Well, It turned out to be that little $5 charger plug all right, but it also included about $7,900 cash. The next week, there was another package that arrived. It had been mangled badly, and the newspaper inside was almost coming out of the little holes in the box. Fortunately, the stuff inside the newspaper wasn't falling out of the box, because there was also $10,000 cash in there. There was a stack of $100 bills that would have choked a fully grown mule.

"So, are you good with the building?"

"Oh my gosh. Yes. Thank you."

"Oh no big deal."

This really kicked our search for a builder into high gear, but now we couldn't find one because everyone we called was booked for a long time. We called erectors from all over Phoenix, and NOBODY we called was available. They were all busy! However, we were able to find a company to do the foundation for us. It's amazing how fast things can get done when you just pay a company to do it. In no time, a beautiful, very thick, perfectly smooth foundation was drying right where the building was going to go.

The day after the foundation had been poured and was curing, I was outside just looking at it and praising God for what He was doing when my next-door neighbor walked over. Our neighbor was a very kind man. He said that he had been looking at the building parts and was certain he could put it together for us. It turns out, that he used to have a job putting those types of buildings together. We asked him if he was interested in the job. He said, "How about $20/hr?". Paul said, "How about $25/hr?" We had a building contractor! The next couple months were amazing. It was a joyful time, and we celebrated all the little things.

Eventually, the building was almost finished. We were excited to show people the finished product. By the time the building had passed all inspections and was finished, we were able to use it to store the stuff from our house while Paul was working on the flooring. Whenever people came over, we would take them outside and tell them the story of the Building that God Built. This was a great miracle. And although I had hoped the building would be used by us for events and projects in Arizona, God had other plans in mind.

Holy Spirit was giving Paul all kinds of energy to fix this and that. Perhaps it was the building getting finished, the newness of a new season, but we were really enjoying our home. We had things in that house that had been broken for years, and now Paul felt compelled to fix them. God was giving me ideas as well. I took on a kitchen project. Sasha, who loves home repair projects, took me out to look at paint. I ended up painting all my kitchen cabinets and walls. It was quite an adventure. It was about this time that our son, Josiah, said that he wanted to be baptized. He was already a believer in Jesus, but he had just never been baptized. We hosted the baptism at our home. It was a wonderful time, even with the wild storm that came in during the baptism.

It was sometime after the baptism that God gave Paul clear direction that our season was done there. He had a dream that we were living in the woods and when he woke up, he had certainty that we were supposed to move. He began to look at land in places where there were lots of trees. He spent most of his time looking at land in the mid-west region. I knew this was a move of God because within the first few weeks of moving into that house many years before, God gave me a dream where I took a tour of a house in the woods and was told we would live there. Also, several years before that, God had shown me a map of several regions one after the other. And thus far, we had lived or been to several of them. The Midwest was one of the regions I had been shown. We didn't have a clue where we would end up in this move, but I knew that it was God's plan. He always provides for His plans.

Without knowing where we were headed, we put the house up for sale. Our home was out in the boon docks of the desert, which made it a very cheap purchase for us. However, through the years of living there, we had developed the land. We had places for animals. We had built a solar array and had powered many things from solar.

We had a newly fixed up house with new flooring and painted walls and cabinets. We had a small shop that we used for many years. And of course, we had a large one that was gifted to us. God had a plan for that building that was bigger than our perception. Because of that building, and the changes we made over those years, our house almost tripled in value.

God found us the just the right buyers for our beloved home. By the time Feast of Tabernacles came, we knew it was our last one there. That Feast of Tabernacles was our most precious in Arizona. Most of our friends came and we celebrated big. We closed on our home sometime after that. The sale enabled us to pay off the remaining mortgage of the home we sold and still have enough left over to buy our next home with cash. This was a special gift for us. About two years before, I had asked God to allow us pay cash for our next home. I love the gifts God gives us. God is good and He is faithful to us in all seasons. Where could we go where He is not there? I am so glad that His thoughts are higher than ours. He gives us His promise. He brings forth help to see it through. He provides the resources for His plans. He's a builder. He shows us what to do and where to go. He is Jehovah Jireh; The Lord always provides for His plans.

Welcome Home

"Now won't God grant justice to his chosen
people who cry out to him day and night? Is
he delaying long over them? I tell you that
he will judge in their favor, and quickly! But
when the Son of Man comes, will he find this
trust on the earth at all?" (Luke 18:7-8, CBJ)

Several years ago, on December 27, 2015, when we lived in Arizona, I had a dream where Paul and I were sitting at a computer desk in a room that was used for storage. In the dream, it was the master bedroom. We were looking at a house in the woods using a laptop that we did not have at the time. I was shown a map in the lower Midwest region where this house was. In the dream, we pushed the "Buy Now" button on the housing website to purchase it and suddenly, the money to pay for it came from our bank account. There was no mortgage. For the longest time, that dream seemed very distant to me. But one day, everything was revealed.

It was probably sometime around 2015 that I began to have several dreams about living in the woods. In one dream, I was taken by an angel to view a house that was surrounded by trees. The angel was dressed like a realtor. Well, he wore a business suit and, somehow, I knew he was my realtor. He ushered me into the house by the front door. The house had a porch and looked very much like a mountain home. There was wood everywhere throughout this home. We walked into a wooded living room and there were some doors leading into other rooms. To the very left was a blue room. To me, this room was something awful. It wasn't a pretty blue at all. I just didn't like that room, and I told the angel that I didn't like it. He just laughed and waved me towards the kitchen in the back. I noticed stairs near the kitchen and wondered what was down there. After that, the angel took me outside where I could see the land. The land was beautiful. I loved the land and I thought to myself, I could live here. When Paul and I finally began to use that storage room as our master bedroom/work room, it dawned on me... The desk space, and the newer laptop we had on it was just like the dream I had. I suspected that at some point in our journey, we would buy a house in the woods. When, I didn't know.

A few more years went by before Paul had a dream about moving. And when he did, I knew it was time. I wasn't sure where we'd end up, but I knew there would probably be a lot of trees. Paul looked at many places from Arkansas through Iowa. One day, a realtor called us and said she'd seen a house that was next to Mark Twain National Forest. She described it and showed us a few pictures she took. We were excited. Paul was excited. It was in the woods, it had land for hunting, a beautiful pond, and a lovely porch. We decided right then and there we would buy that house. We started that process and before we knew it, we sold our house in Arizona, and owned a home in the Midwest, sight unseen! We picked up a friend the day we moved. It was a stray cat that had been starving. The kids fed it and fell in love with him. We decided to take him with us. It was sort of an impulsive decision, but it was a pretty wild and exciting time. We didn't realize how often the cat and our pug would have little slapping battles. We now had two pets, a pug and a stray cat. The kids named him Cat Gut. What a travel adventure that was. Sasha, my good friend, drove the boys and me in our car, while Paul drove our large moving truck, towing our electric car behind it. We stopped at her mom's house on the way.

In 2015, I had several dreams about the details of this move, not only the route that would be taken, but places we'd stop and what we'd do there. One on Christmas eve, one on Christmas day, and another Christmas night. This is part of what I wrote down in my dream tablet from a dream on Christmas night:

> I dreamed my husband Paul, the kids, and I were
> in some city where we were staying with an older

black lady, her white husband, and her daughter. We were just there temporarily and while we were there, Paul was doing some sort of legal work. There was excitement in the air and the kids were having fun. Paul and I were also having fun. We used our free time to do things like find interesting churches, historic buildings, and points of interest like famous hotels.

It was traveling to Sasha's mom's house that jogged my memory of this particular dream. Sasha's mom has some African roots and it turned out that she lives at a historic hotel on Route 66. I didn't really know any of this until we went there. Sasha's mom is very involved at her church and took us there for a Wednesday night service. She introduced us to her pastor, who is white. It was meeting her pastor that made me go and find this dream in my dream journal to reread it. Another interesting thing about this stop is that while we there, we were in the middle of talking with the bank about how we needed to transfer the money to pay for the new house.

When we arrived at our new home, we were not surprised at the beauty of the land. Oh, it was every bit as fabulous as I had seen in pictures and in dreams. But that blue room, there was no getting around it. It was the ugliest room I had ever seen. And, it was the master! The shag carpet in it was so dirty. I vacuumed it over and over, filling up the vacuum each time. Yet, it never got clean. I really did not like that room, but I was so grateful to have a home with such a beautiful view. Our time there was amazing and unforgettable. We shot two deer on our property. We caught fish in our pond, and we took hikes into the woods every day. We also joined a wonderful church. It was a very rural area, but had a strong community of believers. The children's director there was excellent. She did an amazing job helping my youngest son connect.

Paul had started a work project that was bringing us into the Kansas City area. We put our house up for sale and started looking for where we could possibly move. We saw lots of places online and connected with a realtor from Glad Heart reality in Kansas City. Our realtor was very helpful and over the next few months, we drove up to view houses around the outskirts of Kansas City. We were hoping to find a place where we had a little space to grow food and house animals. We looked at several things in our range of budget and finally came across a lovely little house on almost two acres. We were excited to find it. Right away, we planned with our realtor to see it. The day we came to see the house, it was cold and snowy. The house was warm and a perfect size for a family that likes to spend a lot of time together like us. We were excited about the prospect of this house. We prayed and decided to trust God and whatever plans He had for us.

One day, we got a call that our bid was accepted. We were very happy to hear the news, but we still didn't have a buyer for our house near Mark Twain National Forest. We asked the Lord to help us to do what we needed to do the get the house sold. This meant painting, fixing, and, most importantly, renovating that blue room. My realtor in southern Missouri and her mom were so faithful in helping us get that blue room turned around into a beautiful master suite. I am very grateful for their help. Eventually, a buyer came, and we started making plans for packing. My mom and little brother flew over to help us pack the moving truck and just to do some fishing and hiking with us. The day my mom and brother flew back home was the day we were also planning on moving to our new home. We had a fabulous time.

On March 19, 2019, I had two dreams. In the first, we visited my friend Sasha at her place of work, except she wasn't really Sasha. It was a messenger. The workplace had lots of rooms, some with glass windows. These rooms were various ministry opportunities. The messenger, looking like Sasha, said to me, "A storm is coming." In the dream I was so interested in getting to work and getting involved. I understood that this business was Kingdom work for God, and I wanted to be a part it. So, I asked if we could just start working. She told me again that a storm was coming and that I needed to get into the chapel. I noticed a chapel with a larger than life open doorway that had no doors on it. It was always open. Next in the dream, we jumped to what looked like a college dorm. There was a lobby and a sitting room with a television, and in the back, there were lots of rooms that went up several floors. I went into this dorm and went to take my purse (which was covered in flowers in the dream) to Sasha, who was also staying in this dorm. When I put my purse in her room, I didn't see Sasha there.

I noticed that there was a man dressed like a girl in the room. He came across as very perverse in this dream and there was a demonic presence that was overwhelming in that room. I asked the man if he knew Sasha. The man held his head down and said he knew of her. She had been talking to him about Jesus. Then I put my purse down. The man did a surprising thing, he took my purse and wouldn't give it back to me. I was very upset and didn't understand what had just happened. I went out of the dorm looking for my sons. I found my youngest, but my older son was missing. Finally, I found him. I noticed that he only had underwear on and he said that he needed clothes. I was so confused.

We went to the man who wouldn't give me back my purse. I asked him where I could find help for my family. He said he knew where I could get help. He walked me down a road past a train on the tracks. The train was either empowered by the Holy Spirit or was going through an area empowered by the Holy Spirit, because I clearly saw the anointing of God over everything near it. Not far from these tracks was a place with a sign that said Prayer House at the top. I knocked on the door for help. The perverse man told me that a lady who could help me could also be found working down there. He pointed towards an area where there was a large park and lots of people gathered to help us. The man who took my purse began to lead me towards a large group of people. As he walked and got closer to the group, he held his head down in shame. I noticed that Holy Spirit was trying to speak to him. I could tell he didn't want to listen, though he heard every word. As we walked towards the large group, I knew they were all gathered to help me and my family. Then suddenly, I had my purse back. I was excited to get it back. However, when I looked in it, only a few precious items were left in it. I walked in the night with my family following Holy Spirit and said to myself, "I am so unprepared for this." Then I woke up.

On April 3, 2019, Paul took my mom and brother back to the airport up in Kansas City and got a hotel for the night for them to stay in until their early morning flight. He paid for the room for two nights because he was taking them in the 26 foot packed moving truck towing our electric car, and he was going to park it at the hotel while he came back to get us in a rental car. I don't drive anymore ever since driving off the road after going temporarily blind from M.S. symptoms in the Arizona heat. He said his goodbyes to my mom and brother, then drove back to get the kids and me. We were driving our second car up to the hotel the next morning. When we arrived at the hotel, Paul noticed the truck and our car were gone. He drove closer to where he had parked it and noticed broken glass where the driver side door had been. Before he even parked, I got out of the car and went into the hotel to find out where our moving truck was. I wondered if they had it towed. The workers on that shift said they hadn't seen any moving truck there that morning. It hit me like a ton of bricks. This was the storm. The dorm was really this hotel. My purse was really everything we had ever owned, including our home business products which was our only employment at that point and all our work equipment. We were very traumatized.

In addition to our dramatic situation, the family buying our house near Mark Twain National Forest needed more time to close. We were stuck at the hotel, with no money, no possessions, and we weren't even sure if we were going to be able get the house we were trying to get. It was a very overwhelming time for us. After about two days of talking to the police, crying in the hotel room, and long phone calls with my momma, I finally decided to call my realtor at Glad Heart. I told her what happened. She, being a follower of Yeshua prayed with me on the phone. Later she called back and said that her office was also praying for us. We visited our new church for the first time. We went up for prayer at the end and came up to a lady from India. We told her our situation and she proceeded to tell us about when her family moved to the Kansas City area. They had given away all of their possessions before coming. They had no work and no food or anything for their kids. She told us how they had left their apartment to go pray at the prayer room, and came back in a snow storm and found a bunch of food on their porch. She said that for a time, there were many miraculous things that happened. God provided for them in many amazing ways. She said life eventually became more stable. Her husband found work, and things smoothed out. She said that she thought it was going to be like that for us too. She said that in the coming days, very miraculous things were going to happen to us that would be God's provision. Then, after a time, things would stabilize.

My realtor had the idea to start a funding campaign. I really had no clue what would happen with it. This was a really difficult time for my whole family. Even my mom and brother, who so faithfully helped us pack everything, were feeling the trauma. I was reminding myself of God's faithfulness as the days rolled along. We sat in the hotel and recalled the beautiful things God had done for us. We called on every emergency verse we had. I thought about the chapel with the wide doorway with no doors and so we found ourselves at the International House of Prayer near the realtor's office often. It never closes, like a doorway with no doors. My son Josiah regularly recited some of the names of God to me when I would cry, to remind me of who God was while we were staying the hotel. I knew Paul was going through something. After all, his whole livelihood was taken. These were days when we experienced a deep intimacy with Jesus. We just wanted to be held by Him.

News reporters came to interview us at the hotel. I just want to pause, and personally praise God for every reporter and photographer and videographer that spoke to us. They helped us so much. God used them mightily to get the word out to the people of Kansas City and surrounding areas to be on the lookout for our stolen moving truck and car. The news reporters found out about the funding campaign and talked about it on their news stations. There were newspaper articles about our trauma, and people from all over began to, not only give to the funding campaign, but they started calling our realtor with donations of furniture, clothes, dishes, lamps, etc... I really believe that God granted us compassion through the news reporters that interviewed us. Every single one was so kind, and we felt their kindness and desire to help us overcome our trials. We are so grateful for the way they used their resources on our behalf.

Our church down in southern Missouri gave us beautiful financial gift. Our faithful friends from our homeschool group in Maricopa shared their love, encouragement, and prayers with us. Many of our friends from our church in Arizona, and many other friends in Arizona shared resources and prayers. Many of my college friends gave and were praying for us. Our friends from our sons' Children Bible Study Club and our Bible study groups prayed for us and were big-hearted. Our friends and family in Washington were so very generous. Our friends in Africa were praying for us. Our friends and family in Texas were so faithful in sharing with us. We had friends that we hadn't talked to in years from states all over that were so kind and donated to help get us on our feet again. The home school organization for this region in the Midwest donated homeschooling supplies to us. We were daily overwhelmed by abundance and blessings. All the furniture and kitchenware and clothes that we received were so much nicer than anything we ever owned before. The irony of this move is that we didn't even have furniture. All we had were the 60 folding chairs our church in Arizona had given us for celebrating things like Seders. Now we had couches and a kitchen table. Everything in our home now was provided to us by God through the love and compassion of others. When we had nothing, they gave us their best possessions. We got a "Welcome Home" that was beyond anything we could have imagined.

Whenever we had a news interview, I would tell them the dream God gave me and I would tell them that I knew the truck would be found. I had a photographer ask me, "Do you really believe that?" I said with certainty, "Yes, I do!" We saved the list of everyone who helped us, and we pray for all of them. Our house near Mark Twain Forest finally closed, and the owners of the house we bid on held it for us. They even left a washer and dryer, chickens, and some furniture pieces for us. I am very grateful to that family. Everyone that helped us close on the houses gave us gifts. We were overwhelmed with the goodness of God. God's love towards us through everyone far outweighed the sadness and the grief of loss. We got a welcome home that we shall always remember. We experienced in spades the hands and feet of Jesus. I think it's interesting that this was how the Creator chose to birth us into Kansas City. He chose us for that journey. We are so honored that God trusted us with it.

Thinking about what God had shown in the dream, I understand now that the place that was called Prayer House was a location marker for Glad Heart Realty. Glad Heart is right next to a House of Prayer. The lady who I sought out to help us was our wonderful realtor. I pray abundance over her and her family. The large group in the park was our friends and family and all the beautiful people that sacrificed to help a total stranger. I pray that every one of those wonderful people are saturated in the good pleasure of God's love. And the man dressed like a girl, I pray for him all the time. God showed me that he wants Jesus, but feels so much shame. The Lord showed me that Holy Spirit has been speaking to him. I pray that he realizes how valuable he really is to God. I pray that he finds his identity through God's word, not by what he feels. I believe that it is probably a heavy burden to walk around feeling like a thief and being afraid of being caught. I told God that for my retribution for all our trauma, I want that man and his whole household to become fully surrendered followers of Jesus. I plan to talk with this man in heaven about how good God is. You know, the train tracks I never thought about until now. However, after church today we went to a store nearby it to get milk and cereal. On the way out of the parking lot, I saw the train going by. And it dawned on me, there wasn't one thing that God didn't know about concerning what happened to us. He brought us here to Kansas City and gave us a welcome home party that our hearts will always remember.

As for that moving truck, someone wrote on the funding campaign page that they saw it in the woods while picking mushrooms. The police checked it out, and there it was, buried to the axles in mud. It was the Eve of Passover 2019. I told you God gives us gifts around feast seasons. The Kansas City police department are amazing people. From the beginning, they were so faithful to our case and I feel blessed to have had the opportunity to get to know just a few of them. The detective assigned to our case prayed regularly for us.

They were as excited as we were when our truck was found. The man who stole everything took most of our belongings out of the truck. Many things were taken. Many things were destroyed. It didn't matter. I was so blessed to see how beautiful God was to us. He returned to us what was lost. Many things survived. More than half of our family photos, some of my son's baby memories, our deep freezers, some of our books, all of our Bibles and Christian music survived, and all 60 chairs for our feast celebrations remained in the moving truck. They even left almost all of our paintings. However, they did take one. They took our painting of Jesus holding a little boy while lovingly looking into the boy's eyes. It was my favorite painting, and a Christmas gift for our sons one year. I pray that God uses that painting to his glory wherever it is right now. God is faithful and doesn't lie. God is good all the time. After they found our missing moving truck, I sent a text to one of the reporters I had gotten to know. It said, "I got my purse back."

Epilogue

God has called us all by name. Each of our journeys will look different. That's how it's meant to be. My mother-in-law Linda worked at a school many years ago. She noticed that one of the male leaders of the school spent a lot of time with one of the girl students there. Holy Spirit kept nudging Linda to talk to that administrator and question his attachment to that student. God gave Linda the boldness to have a conversation with that leader. The school leader was angry. Rumors spread that Linda was oversensitive and used bad judgement in how she perceived the situation at hand. Linda felt shunned the remaining of her time working under that leader's administration. Many years later, Linda died. It was after her death that we found out that Linda's gut feelings on that leader's behavior were true. The young lady my mother-in-law tried to protect years before confirmed this to my husband's family during our season of bereavement following Linda's passing. That school leader had indeed abused that young lady in her youth. She said that after Linda made such a fuss about how the leader was interacting with her, he never touched her again. Linda had saved that girl without ever knowing she did. Linda simply followed Holy Spirit, even if it cost her reputation and favor from her boss. She didn't fear what others thought of her, because she understood her identity came from God. And by living out her calling, she made more of a difference for the kingdom of God than she realized on Earth. I hope this book helps you on your journey of embracing who the Lord says you are. I also pray that you continue to learn how to hear His voice. May you follow Jesus, no matter the cost. No one is a friend like Jesus. Shalom

Appendix

Pregnant?

Crisis Pregnancy Centers (CPCs) and Pregnancy Resource Centers (PRCs) are not-for-profit organizations that serve women across the United States. They offer life giving options for you and your unborn baby. You are not alone in this.

Find your local CPC by going to www.optionline.org. or calling 1-800-395-4357

Abused?

If anything about my story of abuse resonated with you or seemed painfully familiar in your life, please seek help now.

National Child Abuse Hotline:
1-800-4-A-CHILD
(1-800-422-4453)
National Domestic Violence Hotline: 1-800-799-7233

Want intimacy with Jesus?

Find out more about God's love for you in the Bible. Also, I strongly encourage you to connect with a solid follower of Jesus and build relationship with them and other believers who are also seeking intimacy with Christ.

Want Eternal Life with your Creator?

The following is from PeaceWithGod.net:

We can't earn salvation; we are saved by God's grace when we have faith in His Son, Jesus Christ. All you have to do is believe you are a sinner, that Christ died for your sins, and ask His forgiveness. Then turn from your sins—that's called repentance. Jesus Christ knows you and loves you. What matters to Him is the attitude of your heart, your honesty. We suggest praying the following prayer to accept Christ as your Savior:

> "Dear God, I know I'm a sinner, and I ask for your forgiveness. I believe Jesus Christ is Your Son. I believe that He died for my sin and that you raised Him to life. I want to trust Him as my Savior and follow Him as Lord, from this day forward. Guide my life and help me to do your will. I pray this in the name of Jesus. Amen."

Bibliography

Introduction
Romans 8:35-38 (NLT)

Chapters
1. Falling in Love
    Psalm 56:3 (NKJV)
    Away in A Manger William J. Kirkpatrick (1895) and James Ramsey Murray (1887).
2. Seeds of Learning
    Galatians 6:9 (NIV)
3. Of Spankings and Shopping
    Romans 4:7 (HCSB)
    1 John 3:1 (TPT)
4. Barbie Dolls and Fancy Cars
    Ephesians 1:18-19 (CJB)
5. Play a Game
    1 Peter 4:10 (NIV)
6. Forgotten Daughter
    Isaiah 25:4 (NLT)
    1 John 4:4 (NLT)
    Jeremiah 32:27 (NLT)
7. My Victory Torch
    Matthew 28:19-20 (CEV)
    Matthew 28:19-20
    Pass it On, a song by Kurt Kaiser written in 1969
    Philippians 4:13
    Psalm 139:14
    John 8:36
    Psalm 23:6.

8. My Future Husband
    Psalm 145:18-19 (NIV)
    Acts 19:11 (TPT)
9. The Great Hamster Chase
    Galatians 5:1 (CJB)
10. The Great Escape
    Galatians 5:13 (NIV)
    Isaiah 9:2 (NKJV)
11. Ministry of Friendship
    John 15:12-15 (NIV)
12. Aunties Listening Ear
    Philippians 2:3-4 (TPT)
13. Straight Shooter Mary
    Ephesians 4:15 (CEV)
14. Broken Boy
    Psalm 137:1 (TPT)
15. How to Escape a Fire
    John 14:21 CJB
16. Fathered
    Psalm 118:5 (TPT)
    1 Chronicles 29:14 (HCSB)
    Hebrews 6:10 (HCSB)
    Psalms 10:14 (NIV)
17. Gratitude
    Philippians 4:6-8 (HCSB)
    The Filling Station: Presents Bible Truths For Children with Practical Applications! (2006) [DVD] written by Jane E Dickerson. USA Spoken Word of God Ministries http://www.spokenwordofgod.org/
18. Becoming a Family
    Isaiah 55:8 (NIV)
    Proverbs 3:5-6 (NIV)
19. Waiting in the Miracle
    Isaiah 51:3 (TPT)

Zechariah 14
Matthew 24
Luke 24:50
Matthew 5:3 (CJB)
Easton's Bible Dictionary—Bethany
Hitchcock's Bible Names Dictionary—Bethany
Smith's Bible Dictionary—Bethany
International Standard Bible Encyclopedia—Bethany
https://theopolisinstitute.com/the-meaning-of-the-mount-of-olives/

30   The Building God Built
     Psalm 50:10-12 (NASB)
31   Welcome Home
     Luke 18:7-8 (CBJ)

About the Author

Barbara Holmes is a daughter of the Most High, a beloved wife of Paul, an active homeschool mama, and a blessed grandmama. She is a survivor of sexual, physical, and mental childhood abuse, who overcame by the word of God, the guidance of the Spirit of God, and help from Bible-grounded counsel. She has labored in many fields associated with the education of children and young adults throughout her life. She is an advocate for children, both born and unborn. Her personal goal in life is that everyone she encounters will walk away knowing they are completely loved by Jesus.